Uncle Otto's Puppet Theatre

UNCLE·OTTO'S PUPPET·THEATRE
A JEWISH FAMILY SAGA

Brigid Grauman

Cover design by Lewis Heriz
Formatting by Anessa Books

ISBN: 9781697102154

Contents

For my father

This book has had a long gestation. I started it way before my father Bob died, and I finished it several years after. In many ways, it is a homage to him. Two people helped me get there thanks to their constant support. First my husband, Giles Merritt, who told me I could do it, and who read the manuscript more than once with a clear and discerning eye. And then Cleveland Moffett who over the many years of our friendship has always encouraged my writing. I owe them both a great debt of gratitude. My sisters Lucy and Tessa were enthusiastic readers, as were my cousins Frank and Thomas. Thank you all very much.

Prologue

A comic play and seven memoirs

My ancestors were all migrants. On my mother's side, they left grinding poverty in Ireland for slightly less grinding conditions in Manchester, where they worked in the cotton mills. On my father's side, poverty and persecution drove them from Slovakia and Galicia in the east of the Austro-Hungarian Empire, to Moravia, now in the Czech Republic. Later, like thousands of Moravian Jews, many of my forebears moved to Vienna or Prague.

These were poor people, and yet by the late 19th century both sides of the family had climbed the social ladder with remarkable speed. My Irish grandfather went from the poorhouse to become Ireland's first ambassador to Great Britain. My Czech grandfather, who had grown up above his father's small shoemaking shop in Brno, became an international lawyer in Vienna.

The migrations didn't end there. As a young woman, my mother uprooted herself from her native London, fleeing a catholic childhood and incurable grief over her dead sister. She was to end her days as a magazine editor in Brussels. As for my Viennese-born American father Bob, he spent the greatest part of his life in France. Asked where he felt most at home, he would reply France, the United States and Vienna, in different ways and for different reasons.

I don't know whether my parents suffered from not having a real home, or if having a real home even matters. My own sense of Jewishness is rooted in a feeling of not belonging anywhere, which is one definition among hundreds of what it is to be a Jew. This is not unpleasant. An Irish passport, Jewish origins, born in Geneva, long years in Belgium, bilingual... My half-sister Diane, who is French, is defiantly uninterested in ancestry. She is her own construction. "Is your book in French?" she asked, and when I told her that it was not, she said, "Good, then I won't have to read it!"

Whereas I have always wanted to hear my parents tell me about their childhoods. I am a journalist whose working life centres on listening to people, and making stories out of what I hear. Reconstructing my family's history has been a similar exercise. It has allowed me to create my backstory and this has given me foundations, or a more serene view of my rootless life.

I have accumulated no less than seven memoirs by family members, which I believe to be an unusual haul. These aren't diaries, but books with a narrative intention. All of them belong to my paternal grandmother's side of the family, as these were the relatives who survived the Second World War. Although each of these memoirs is different in tone and intention, their authors were all foreigners in lands where they never came to feel fully integrated. Each of their stories tries to make sense of the writer's destiny, and does so by recalling worlds that had long disappeared.

The year after my father, Robert (Bob), died, my three sisters and I decided that as a way of staying close once a year we would meet for a long weekend in a French spa town. Two of us live in Brussels, the other two in Paris. We speak to each other in French when the four of us are together. Enjoying this unusual adventure, we have gorged on oysters at Le Touquet, sunned beside the mountain lake at Aix-les-Bains, and walked along Trouville's beach with its long row of timbered houses.

None of us lived with our father beyond the age of ten. He had parted from his first two wives, and stayed with his third wife until his death aged almost 84. He became an American citizen in his late teens, but France was the country he knew best. Twice married to French women, his insights into that country were always those of an outsider. Despite a mysteriousness about him, an elusiveness we never quite pierced, there is a little "Bobness" in each of us.

Bob said one day of my French niece Marina who lives and works in Rouen: "That my granddaughter deals with non-contentious civil law in Normandy would have been astonishing to my parents. A French provincial town is so remote from anything they knew." Although he was marvelling at his fate, the unexpected twists and turns of migration are what societies and identity are all about. Most of us can look back at our ancestors' criss-crossings of the globe when, like millions of migrants, they tried to find better lives.

I keep the seven memoirs in a large black box in my office. The first I read was my grandmother's, then my uncle's, and after that the one by my father's cousin Bus. When I started writing about Vienna, Prague and Brno, my father put his own recollections down on paper. After that I discovered memoirs penned by his uncle Richard, who although a minor figure on Vienna's cultural scene had been a very big name among translators of Shakespeare into German.

The memoirs by my father's cousin Peter came to me by chance, and opened up a secret door to a story I had known nothing about. The last of the memoirs was by Peter's father, Otto, the portrait painter. Peter had sent me the battered red folder through the post with a note saying I was welcome to it. He didn't want it back because it mentioned neither his mother nor himself, and that was all that interested him. Oddly enough, all these memoirs are in English, except for my grandmother's in German. Together they form a remarkable gift from the past, and an irresistible invitation to explore the worlds my family had belonged to.

In his novel *Der Weg ins Freie* (The Road into the Open), Arthur Schnitzler depicted characters incarnating the many forms of Jewishness among the early 20th-century Vienna bourgeoisie, from self-hating Jew to Zionist, from culture lover to social snob. Like these, my family reflected many expressions of Jewish self-identification, including my grandfather's distaste for everything Jewish.

Being a Jew was never easy because of other people's prejudices, even those of Jews. In 2019, unbelievably, primitive forms of anti-semitism have reemerged across Europe, notably in the UK, France, Hungary and Poland. Even in relatively tolerant Belgium, a carnival float in a Flemish town that year featured Orthodox Jews sitting on bags of money, a rat on one man's shoulder. According to the organisers, this was a light-hearted joke, not to be taken seriously.

Perhaps the spectre of anti-semitism never goes away, and testimony to my fears that this may be so, here is the story of an ordinary family of Jews, and how they lived their lives over almost two centuries.

-1-

1932: The puppet theatre's one and only musical comedy

Summer 1932, a sunny Sunday afternoon in Austria. The political mood is tense as Adolf Hitler's growing popularity in Germany is already casting its shadow, and the Great Depression that followed World War One is still at the root of job losses and soaring inflation. But largely untouched by these troubles, the sprawling monastery and imperial palace of Klosterneuburg, a small town on the Danube upriver from Vienna, typify the benevolent Catholicism introduced in the 12th century by Leopold the Good, Austria's patron saint.

The scene opens in the living room of a three-storey villa secluded behind a stone wall. The wall hides a garden of chestnut and linden trees, and an orderly flowerbed of petunias and dahlias. Inside, the furniture is functional rather than stylish. Six-year-old Bob, the child of the house, is racing up and down excitedly. "Hush!" his mother Emma says.

Otto, handsome in his late thirties, shirtsleeves rolled up, has with the help of his sister Emma heaved the oak table across the room and plonked it next to the piano. He now stands behind it, ready for the performance. With cardboard, pencils, watercolours, scissors and glue, he had made a puppet theatre the day before in his studio in Döbling. It stands on the table, the size of three shoeboxes piled one on top of the other.

Emma and her husband, Arthur, had moved to Klosterneuburg, away from Vienna's pollution and its threats of latent violence. She had grown up in Vienna with Otto and their three other siblings, upstairs from the family's brandy bar. That summer morning Otto had caught the train to Klosterneuburg from Döbling with his girlfriend and his small son, past the Karl-Marx-Hof in the Heiligenstadt suburb on the Danube, the most impressive of hundreds of new communal housing projects funded by Vienna's socialist government.

Self-portrait: Otto's expression says much about the turn of events in 1932 Vienna

Otto was proud of Red Vienna, and increasingly alarmed by the reactionary pressures threatening the Austrian capital's socialist administration. In May, the right-wing Catholic politician Engelbert Dollfuss had become Chancellor of Austria, and the Nazi menace was starting to undermine the socialist movement.

The Klosterneuburg living room – Turkish carpets, oak furniture, comfortable armchairs, Otto's paintings – is the regular setting for musical get-togethers with friends from Vienna. For this more intimate event, Bob's grandmother Josefine has arrived in a taxi. "*Ich küsse Ihre Hand,*" says

Emma. Wearing a dirndl, her dark wiry hair pulled back in a knot, Emma has baked the nut cake lying on the sideboard. Bob wishes his mother's dirndl didn't strain so over her bosom. His father Arthur is elegant as ever, sporting a tie.

Otto's girlfriend is a concert pianist who also composes light music. She tours with the famous violinist Alma Rosé, Mahler's niece who was to die at Auschwitz after having led a women's orchestra there. When Hilde's long, tapered fingers touch the Bösendorfer grand's keyboard, Otto raises the cardboard curtain and they start to sing to the audience seated before them.

First cousin lookalikes: my father Bob, left, and Peter

The play's first act takes place at Klosterneuburg's beach in a bend of the Danube, where in the summer Viennese weekenders float in the green waters, and many have little summer cottages. Otto slides his cardboard figures across the stage thanks to parallel slits in the floor, and his backdrops circle an oblong shaft. Hilde has written the music, and Otto the libretto. A pert cardboard Bob appears in white shorts, joining his father who is frowning, arms crossed. Bob wants a car. "*Ich möchte einen grossen roten!*" (I want a large red one), announcing that he's ordered a driver's license through the post.

Against a backdrop depicting a house interior, a red-nosed postman appears clutching an envelop, which grandmother Josefine grabs and confiscates, knowing what it contains. The audience particularly enjoys this joke because when she visits Klosterneuburg, Josefine invariably turns up in an ancient pre-World War One Phänomen taxi with outside gearshift and handbrake, driven by a very old man. She doesn't trust any driver under sixty. Meanwhile on stage, a chauffeur turns up in a green jacket, blond hair centrally parted and slicked down.

The story becomes increasingly absurd, involving giants, singing gherkins, two gossiping pigeons, a wizard wearing a fez, a village simpleton with pudding-basin haircut. Otto masterminds a frenzied wild goose chase in front of rapidly changing scenery, a village, the forest, the depths of the Danube, a concert hall, simultaneously producing sound effects with a bucket filled with water and by striking spoons on saucepans. The boys, and indeed the whole family, are clutching their sides with laughter.

In the play's general tumult, the chauffeur-driven car crashes, and a bald policeman appears in blue cap and jacket, a truncheon dangling from his belt. With his whiskers and jowls, he is the play's most comic figure. He sings about law and order, until a rumpus erupts at the side of the stage. "I'll sort this out in one second," he yells, heading for the noise. Moments later, cap and uniform askew, he returns on wobbly legs: "*Jetzt hab' ich's ihnen g'zeigt!*" Now I've shown them! The performance goes down so well it has to be repeated all over again. Then Emma makes coffee, and they take the cakes out into the garden and have *Jause*, Austrian high tea.

The plot is inspired by a minor family drama. Buying the family's first car after the move from Vienna made sense as it was more practical for Arthur to drive in to work than catch the train. He had taken driving lessons, and bought a second-hand green Steyr. Built like a tank, this sturdy, unheated square box had a cloth roof that could be raised when it rained, and that in winter was replaced by a hard top. Despite the driving lessons, and to Bob's chagrin as he couldn't think of his father as anything less than perfect, Arthur frequently scraped the bodywork against walls and the garage door.

After the first winter, Arthur bought a Steyr 100, a streamlined sedan with wind-up windows and heating, which Emma also learned to drive. This was a more comfortable car, better suited to the cold months. But then he suddenly announced that he had traded this one in for a third model, the four-cylinder engine, four-speed gearbox Steyr 200.

Emma said Arthur was behaving like a rich man. He argued that the investment represented a major saving. "*Nuh ya*," she complained, "I know he makes a good living, but in the meantime families live in damp tenements infested with rats." Cars were an infrequent sight on Austrian roads, and punctured frequently because of nails and sharp stones. To Bob, who loved engines, watches, fountain pens, anything smooth and well-made, this was the most beautiful object he had ever seen. He loved the new car's smell of fresh rubber, and the purr of its engine.

Otto and Hilde's puppet theatre was partly a

tease, partly a defuser of tensions. Yet it has survived for eighty-five years and is now in my hands. Although it was never intended to last, it did so through the upheavals of exile after my family fled Vienna. And the funny thing is that five of the family members who wrote memoirs feature in its one and only play.

As for Arthur's Steyr 200, after the Anschluss it was confiscated by storm troopers who banged on the front door in Klosterneuburg and told Arthur to hand over the keys. This Arthur immediately did. Bob was startled to see his father so meek. As Arthur was a Czech citizen, the Czech Embassy had the car returned quickly, but to Bob it had lost all its charm. "It smelled of beer and had stains on the seat and carpet. It had been desecrated, violated and its mystery destroyed."

When I take that joyful afternoon in Vienna down from where it lies on top of a row of books, remove the box's cover and look at the drawings inside, I feel a rush of nostalgia for a family I never knew. Inside are the cardboard figures, backdrops and props my great-uncle Otto Flatter had cut out and painted with watercolours that summer day before the Second World War. This cardboard toy is as close as I will ever get to experiencing with the touch of my fingers what it meant to be a Jewish family before the Holocaust.

-2-

A playful afternoon stored for eighty years

Ours was a large family with uncles, aunts and cousins in Vienna, Brno and Prague, and its share of intermarriages. They belonged to a middle-class way of life that involved heavy central European meals, going for hikes in forests and mountains, listening to music, and seeing a lot of one another, even if they didn't always get along, and frequently sulked. All were uneasy with the growingly uncertain political situation after the First World War, and each reacted differently to the fact that they were Jews.

My father Bob, who became an American, liked to tell me about this puppet theatre of his childhood. I had imagined that it resembled a miniature 19th-century theatre, and when I heard that Bob's cousin Ernest in Cardiff, known as Bus, still had it I knew this called for a trip across the English Channel.

Bus lived in a suburban house with a vast swimming pool at the back, a reminder of his youth as an Olympic swimmer on the Czech national team. His wife had died a few years earlier, and weeds grew out of the cracks in the empty pool's concrete walls. The once lush rose garden lay untended, the rose bushes shrivelled and brown. Inside, on the living room walls and in the hall, were family portraits by Otto.

Widows from Cardiff's Jewish community brought Bus home-cooked dishes, but he had no intention of breaking his solitude and getting married again. He called his daughter Frankie in London every day, worked at the local library and took part in amateur theatrics. Despite his age, close to 90, he was in excellent health, a fact he ascribed to a lifetime of swimming and to never taking pills.

I stayed for the weekend, sleeping in the single bed of Frankie's childhood. Bus had made goulash ahead of my visit, and apple strudel. I bought a bottle of red wine down the road, and we ate in the kitchen. Later we settled in the living room, lights dimmed, and I listened to Bus talk about his parents and other relatives, enjoying the rhythm of his Czech accent that was different from my father's slight German cadence.

Guardian of the puppet theatre Bus

When he opened the sideboard and brought out the puppet theatre, spreading it on the table before us, my first feeling was one of disappointment. There was less of it than I had expected. It had no stage, no columns or curtains, no proscenium arch, no outside structure. Only the painted scenery remained and a few props attached to greying string. But my interest quickened when we looked at the characters Otto had drawn. The haughty old woman was my great-grandmother, my grandmother Emma in the yellow dress; my grandfather Arthur with a salt-and-pepper thatch on his head. There was Otto himself in a painter's smock, his girlfriend Hilde wearing lipstick, his playwright brother Richard looking down thoughtfully, and Bob, a grinning boy in swimming trunks.

Bus could remember the play's opening scene at the beach on the Danube where Emma would take the boys to swim. "Emma had knitted her own very unbecoming woollen bathing costume," he said, chuckling. "She was notoriously thrifty. We children also wore horrible woollen trunks that clung to you and never dried."

The play was a musical comedy and Bus remembered Emma's little song:

> *Ich bin die Emma frish und froh,*
> *im selbst gestriktem schwimm tricot*
> I am Emma fresh and gay,
> in the swimming tricot knitted by me

Otto's portraits of a melancholy Emma, left, and their authoritarian mother Josephine

I had read Bus's memoir long before this visit, but I wanted this old man with the freckled skin, whitening moustache and hooded eyes behind large horn-rimmed glasses to tell me stories in his own voice. Once started, he could talk uninterruptedly, as if he had a well of memories inside him overflowing with his younger days, his parents, his schooling, the family business, who in the family felt Jewish.

"How Jewish do *you* feel?" I asked.

"I've never been religious, although I own a good collection of kipas," he said. "I went along to synagogue to make my wife happy." But he felt at home in Cardiff's Jewish community.

"You see, I don't believe in God, but then as a stranger in this country I have always felt more comfortable with Jewish people than with the Welsh or the English. I know what they think. They are familiar. And they have in common that they don't belong anywhere."

I barely knew my father's family, as there were no relatives near Geneva where my sister Lucy and I grew up. The first time I met Bus I must have been around 20. I'd always known that Bus's parents had been taken from Prague to a concentration camp where they were killed.

They, like most of our Czech relatives, had felt safer than they should have, and then it was too late. "I try not to think about what happened," Bus said. "It's a black hole and I don't want to look down it."

In 2010, a few months after my father died, a memorial event was held in Paris. It took place in a hall close to the Protestant church to which his wife belonged. Many people he had known were surprised to hear that Bob had "*des origines juives*". The truth is that, unlike Bus, Bob had never felt Jewish, and didn't feel a sense of familiarity among Jews. He told me that he didn't like mentioning that he was Jewish because he didn't want to be seen as a victim. A Jewish man of his age born in Vienna usually had a tragic story to tell, and he wanted no pity or compassion.

Bus and he were first cousins twice over - two brothers had married two sisters – but despite the double kinship they weren't alike. Bob was a man of the world, thrice married, who could navigate smoothly through different milieux. Bus was a homebody who enjoyed making and fixing things, and cooking "like a real Jewish mama," as he said. He had learned to make strudel in their grandmother's kitchen in Vienna, how to stretch the dough over the side of the table until the long translucent film could be lifted and folded over the raisin- and apple filling.

By today's standards, ours was a highly literate family. No less than seven relatives wrote memoirs, including Bus and Bob. I have them all, along with many black-and-white photographs, and letters that include two long ones written in slanting Gothic script by my great-grandmother Josefine. Some of Otto's paintings have pride of place on my walls in Brussels.

Bus died in 2013. I had wanted to bring the family back to life long before his daughter Frankie in England sent me the puppet theatre, packed in a large flat chocolate box. The puppet theatre and the memoirs and pictures I have collected represent nuggets of ancestry. From these I have teased out real-life people, knowing I have reinvented them, and made them think things *I* believe they would have thought. I realise they might not recognise themselves or each other in my reconstructions. But I have made them mine, and for me that has been like building foundations underneath what had been a flimsy wood cabin.

When Otto constructed the puppet theatre, the men and women of our family were doing well. My great-grandparents had been poor Moravian villagers, but this was an upwardly mobile Jewish family and in Vienna, Prague and Brno their sons became confident professionals with so many relatives that they didn't know them all. To my sister Lucy and me with our small spread-out family, that notion seems an unbelievable luxury.

At the time of leaving Vienna, my grandmother Emma had also packed the script, but this was lost along the way to New York. It may perhaps still lie somewhere in vast vaults on Ellis Island where it was confiscated by the immigration authorities, along with letters and diaries. Otto had brought the theatre itself to London, and when old gave it to his nephew Bus who packed it carefully away in plastic folders marked with each character's name, storing it in a sideboard among other traces of his past.

-3-

1861: Lomnice, land of milk and honey

Out of curiosity I made an appointment with a reform rabbi in Brussels. Technically I am not Jewish as the patrilineal line was recognised only in the very early days of Judaism. Rabbi Nathan Alfred, with well-intentioned blue gaze, said that even the reform community would expect me to convert if I wanted to be a Jew. I had known he would say something along those lines, but still I felt rejected. If I was curious to know what "Jewish" means to a secular Israeli, he recommended I read *jews and words* (sic) by the Israeli writer Amos Oz and his daughter Fania Oz-Salzberger.

As a child of divorce I have spent a great deal of time trying to understand my parents. When I was working as a journalist in Brussels, I would leap at the chance to be alone with Bob. He'd suggest we meet up in Vienna, and we'd stay at a Benedictine hotel where each Spartan room had a Bible in the bedside table drawer and a plain wooden crucifix above the bed. The reason we stayed in that particular hotel is that the upmarket school he attended, the Schottengymnasium, belongs to the same order and is part of the same building complex.

I felt close to Bob when he told me about his childhood, as if our childhoods were the strongest bond between us. I loved how he told memories from a child's perspective, flutters of moments long gone that included those afternoons when the puppet theatre was brought out for a performance. But I also wanted to understand what exile had meant for my family, and if it had made them feel differently about being Jewish. It must at least have made them think about it.

Bob's grandparents were all born in mid-19th-century Moravia, within a half-hour's drive from one another. One place there more than any other has come to embody our family's origins, the small town of Lomnice, where my maternal great-grandfather Siegmund Flatter was born in 1861. Lomnice is idyllically rural, set in hills and woods, and its Jewish quarter has changed so little since the 18th century that it's easy to visualise what it looked like when Siegmund was born, the youngest child of artisan wool merchants.

An Austrian crown land to the east of Bohemia in what is now the Czech Republic, Moravia was renowned for a fine, carded cloth much admired in England and exported across Europe and to Russia, as well as North and South America. Many Jews were involved in the trade. They bought the raw wool from the farms, had it cleaned, woven into cloth and made into fringed, embroidered shawls that fashionable women wore as coats or used as bedspreads. Every few weeks, wagons piled high with bales of cloth left Lomnice for Brno.

Lomnice's Jews first settled there in the early 18th century; the story goes that its feudal lord and his noble counterpart in nearby Lysice exchanged two Jewish families against two dogs. The Jewish part of town was not a real ghetto like those of Poland, but a heavy chain was raised at night to separate the Jews from the Christian quarter. My grandmother Emma remembered examining the holes in walls where the chains had once been driven.

The houses of the Jewish community and an early temple were built of wood; a 1766 petition asked for permission to rebuild the women's ritual bathhouse, the *mikvah*, because it had been eaten away by woodworm and the women had to go to another village to wash. In 1798, when the Austro-Hungarian Empire enforced residential restrictions on Jews, Lomnice had 56 Jewish families - 606 people and a rabbi.

Emperor Joseph II's Edict of Tolerance in 1782 accorded fairer rights to all Austria-Hungarian citizens. Jews were now allowed to lease land, work in trade and industry, and attend state schools. They were also required to register under a German surname; until then they had been son-of or daughter-of.

Why did my family choose the name Flatter? In German, the closest word is *Flattern*, as in the fluttering of a butterfly. I suppose it was my grandmother Emma's joke that the name might have evolved from the Spanish word Flato, or fart. I'm not even sure the family had Sephardic roots; Austrian Jews liked to believe they had origins in liberated Spain rather than in the miserable ghettos of the East. My 92-year-old cousin Felix in London who until recently was the family's oldest survivor, suggested *flatterhaft*, meaning fickle, and *Flattermann*, meaning wanderer.

The wave of revolution that swept across Europe in 1848, seriously shaking the monarchies although not unsettling the Habsburgs, saw Joseph II introduce his wide-ranging reforms. Before that, a set of laws known as the Familiant Laws regulated how many Jews were allowed to have families in the Czech lands of Moravia, Bohemia and Silesia. In Moravia, the maximum was 5,400 families.

If a Jew wanted to marry and start a family he had to have a *Familiennummern* (a family number). These numbers were inherited by eldest sons, with richer families sometimes buying marriage permits for a second or third son. Many Jews married secretly, and their children were illegitimate. They could not settle and were destined to wander about the country, often as beggars.

Siegmund's father must have been an eldest son and was legitimately able to found a family. He inscribed the names and birthdates of each of his children - three boys, seven girls - on the front leaf of his Bible. They had German names and spoke German at home, although the peasants and craftsmen they lived among spoke Czech. Joseph II had established schools where Jews were taught in German, as a way of binding any future elite to Vienna, which is why so many Czech Jews chose that language over Czech. They also felt safer under the Emperor's protection. Equal rights only came to Jews in 1867, a few years after Siegmund was born.

I imagine the floor in my family's small house was of beaten earth. They must have heated the room with log fires and drawn their water from the well, and I can't believe they had the space for more than two beds, if that, and yet they were not considered poor. They had a wool business, selling embroidered tablecloths, bedspreads and shawls to shops in Brno and Vienna, as well as a potash plant, which mined salt for fertiliser. A photograph, my great-great-grandmother wearing a necklace, had them looking quite well-to-do.

But Siegmund's fondly remembered childhood was to be cut short. One fateful market day in Brno, his elder brother Moric gambled the money he had earned from selling a wagonful of cloth and lost it all, as well as his gold watch, his overcoat, the rented wagon and the two borrowed horses. This was a tragedy. Rather than face bankruptcy, his father reimbursed the debts, but all the family's economies were gone.

Both parents fell ill in quick succession and died. Moric left home in shame, and most of the other siblings were old enough to seek work in nearby Brno, or further afield in Vienna. Siegmund was still a child. The story of his stolen childhood was to haunt his children. Each of them evoked it in their memoirs, and each always referred to Siegmund with devotion and love.

Lomnice became Siegmund's paradise lost, and he took his children there when they were young. He said no place could boast sweeter honey or juicier sausages. His painter son Otto wrote about Lomnice many years later, when he was an old man in London. Thinking of the Moravian countryside would draw him vividly back there. "I walk up the hills, I feel the heat reflected from the chalky country lanes, I smell the dunged fields, the mushrooms in velvety undergrowth, I hear the rush of the brook, the lament of a distant accordion and I touch the cool apples hanging from laden trees. I rest and dream in the woods."

The orphaned Siegmund stayed in Lomnice for a while, fed and housed by family and neighbours, but taken in by no one as homes were small. He slept on flea-infested animal skins in a neighbour's storeroom, but every morning went to school where he learned to read and write. After two years living with a housemaid sister in Brno, he was sent aged 13 to Vienna. His brother Henrich, who was working for a sausage maker, had found him an apprenticeship with an upholsterer and wall-paperer.

In the spring of 1994, Bob and I made one of our journeys to central Europe, this time meeting in Brno. We had booked a room in a Soviet-style hotel, and went for an evening meal of roast goose and *knödel*, the sort of fattening food we both loved. We ate cake for dessert. The next morning, we hired a car and drove through the deep-green hilly landscapes of pine forests and cultivated land to Lomnice, hemmed in by fields, orchards and the dense oak trees.

Unlike Vienna, Lomnice has been no more than grazed by time. On its highest hill stands a double onion-dome church and a little lower down a much-reconstructed early Gothic castle where Lomnice's squire used to live. The Jewish quarter at one side of the small town is little more than a somnolent square—Zidovske namesti or Jewish square—planted with horse chestnuts and linden trees and surrounded by one- and two-storey houses painted yellow, ochre and pumpkin. A bust on a pedestal commemorates the turn of the 20th-century Czech author Josef Uher who wrote about the local weavers and died young. The synagogue at one end looks too large for the countryside setting. On an earlier visit it had been grubby and rundown, but this time it was spruced up and painted white.

The three-table restaurant in the middle of a massive white building on the square was closed. We looked at the house where my great-grandfather was born at one side of the synagogue - square-shaped and steep-roofed with ochre-painted walls.

"How could twelve people have fitted in?" I

asked Bob. "God knows," he replied. Pointing at a small bicycle lying on the ground in the yard, my father said, "Now it's probably occupied by a farmer and his wife and child."

The most affecting site in Lomnice is its Jewish cemetery, a stroll down a pebbled path that starts off at one corner of the main square. We took the path and entered the cemetery through a wrought-iron gate set in a long brick wall. Nestled on a steep triangle of grass, it is an untouched place of gentle ghosts. The gravestones jut higgledy-piggledy out of the grass, some large, others small, some with Hebrew lettering carved into the stone. Others are sunken and covered with lichen and weeds, a few inscribed in German on black marble, like that of Moric Flatter.

"Dad, look at this one, could that be the wicked son who gambled away all the money?" Bob stood next to me to look at the pompous marble stone. "He died too late, the dates don't work. Who could he have been?"

We scrambled up and down the steep, overgrown slope, reading out inscriptions, enjoying the smell of grass and warm weather, the chirping of insects and birds. "Zeizl!" Bob cried. "That's family. Emma used to mention them."

People don't usually laugh in cemeteries, but we were elated, and completely alone. The countryside appeared deserted. I suppose the farmers were in the fields and others at work in their shops. "I love this place," Bob said, drawing a deep breath, his hands in his pockets, and looking out over the orchards and hills. He wore a pale blue shirt, and his eyes were the same colour. "I don't know a more peaceful place on earth."

When he was young, his mother Emma and her sister Klara would rent two adjacent houses for the summer. They would bathe with their boys in the swimming baths by the river, and eat at the tavern. They would go for long walks in the forests where they might come across Otto wearing a floppy hat, a canvas propped up on an easel, or they might buy a sandwich of dark bread

Otto might be found at work in Lomnice's meadows or hills

spread with pungent cheese at the stall along the road, or the rock-like nougat made of sugar, honey and almonds that had to be chipped at with a wooden mallet.

It was noon by the time Bob and I returned to the main square, and the restaurant had opened. Two tables stood outside in the sun and we sat down to order omelettes, goulash and salad with a sweet, watery dressing. "Emma used to make the same," Bob said. I still remember that remark years later each time I eat salad with a watery dressing, one of the hundreds of tiny brush strokes that make up my impressionistic memory of Bob's childhood.

We'd paid for the meal and coffee and were planning to drive back to Brno and take a train from there to Prague when suddenly a man in a black suit and felt hat ran across the square to disappear inside the synagogue. "Dad, did you see that? An Orthodox Jew! That's unbelievable. Let's follow him," I said.

We went over to the synagogue and pushed open the heavy pinewood door. Inside the man was talking to another darkly clad man wearing a skullcap, a *yarmulke*. "Hello, I am the deputy mayor of Lomnice, can I help you?" a third man in a suit asked Bob in German, explaining that we had arrived minutes before the official opening of the synagogue as a cultural centre, a project funded by the municipality and the Czech Ministry of Culture.

"The most peaceful place on earth": Bob in Lomnice's country cemetery

He invited us to look around the exhibition on the white-washed walls about the history of Lomnice's Jews. There were sepia photographs and postcards, and a cadastral map dating back to the turn of the 20th century where Siegmund's house was numbered 35 out of 235. The exhibition did not mention Lomnice's most famous Jews: Fanny Neuda, born in 1819, a rabbi's daughter who wrote a bestselling book of prayers for women, and Leo Eitinger, born a century later, an Auschwitz survivor who became a Norwegian psychiatrist specialised in delayed reaction to traumatic experiences, in particular concentration camps.

When we went outside we found men, and a few women and children, standing in the sunshine to one side of the synagogue, their backs to Siegmund's childhood home. They were villagers waiting for the inaugural speeches. The two rabbis, the deputy mayor and a man from Prague's cultural ministry wearing jeans came out and stood in a row. Each made a brief speech. We stood at the back and listened without understanding, as they were speaking Czech.

A plaque to the memory of the victims of the Nazi genocide was unveiled, dedicated to the 58 Jews who still lived in Lomnice between 1939 and 1945 and were killed by the Nazis. I thought how strange it was that Bob was a direct link to those days when Lomnice had a thriving Jewish population living and working alongside Christians, and yet preserving their religious tradition. And that by chance we happened to be here on this occasion. And that nobody knew this but us.

A few months after Bob died in November 2009, my sister Lucy and our half-sister Tessa travelled to Lomnice after a night in Vienna at the austere Schotten hotel with its crucifixes above the beds. Ours was a mini-pilgrimage in memory of our father's roots in central Europe. He had been cremated in the south of France, where he had spent his later years. He had lived in many places and visited many more, but Lomnice harked back to summer holidays when he played brown and barefoot in the fields.

I had badly wanted my sisters to come here. It was raining, the drops softly wetting our cheeks like tears. We squelched down to the cemetery which Bob had thought one of the most beautiful places on earth. When the rain stopped we sat on the grass, talked about him, laughed, felt sad, and drank beer and ate goulash in the tavern from where he and I had spotted the rabbi. "We had to do this," said Lucy. "We had to pay homage to Dad's Jewish roots. They were as much part of him as everything else."

-4-

1873: Early days in Vienna

I have visited Vienna many times, alone to write articles; with friends and with Bob to walk among the ghosts of his past. The public transport system is clean and easy to use, the parks well tended, the buildings almost defiantly well maintained.

Bob loved this chocolate box Vienna.

"My parents would have been astounded if they could see Vienna now," he would say. "It used to be so dirty, beggars everywhere, men missing limbs."

When my great-grandfather Siegmund arrived in 1873 with two *groschen* in his pocket, it was one of the dual monarchy's two capitals. The Austro-Hungarian Empire was second only in size to Russia. The Ringstrasse was still under construction as was Emperor Franz Joseph's ambitious complex of monumental buildings intended to glorify his empire. There is not one architectural masterpiece among them, but their cumulative power still impresses.

The Vienna of those days was an endless worksite. The Burgtheater took 16 years to complete. The Town Hall, modelled on Brussels' Gothic Town Hall but far larger, had been started but would not be finished until ten years later. The "stage set decorations of a vacuous time" was Robert Musil's verdict in his novel *The Man Without Qualities*. Private mansions were going up for the new bourgeoisie, among them many Jews. Vienna's street plan has barely changed since the last year of Empress Maria Teresa's reign, in 1870. Its radial structure still leads from the centre where the noblemen had their palaces out through the middle- and working-class suburbs all the way to the Vienna woods.

Siegmund would have headed for the working-class Vortstadt, the outer reaches of the city where a few dairy farms, market gardens and vineyards were resisting against the rapidly encroaching textile mills, chemical plants and hundreds of small workshops inside residential housing blocks. The housing shortage was acute, as immigrants were pouring in to Vienna from across the empire. Rooms in tenements were rented for rates their tenants couldn't afford. In the Vortstadt, building work was ongoing on a channel to bring the mighty Danube closer to Vienna, and thus stop the devastating floods.

On a cold and drizzly first of May 1873 in the Prater Park, the Emperor officially opened his grandiose World's Fair to herald many confident years of prosperity and growth. The first visitors mingled with the workers because some of the pavilions were not yet finished. The Fair's centrepiece was the Rotunda, a circular structure of wood and iron with an enormous dome, designed by a Scottish engineer. It was a fire hazard that burned down in 1937 in an inferno of molten metal and melted glass that lasted for many days. Bob's cousin Peter went to school close to the Prater, and stood by among crowds watching the roaring orange blaze.

The Rotunda was the centrepiece of Vienna's World's Fair

The fair was to be a financial disaster. A week after its opening, May 9, Vienna's stockmarket collapsed, marking the start of the financial crisis know as the Panic of 1873, which hit New York that September. People panicked in the streets as private fortunes were lost and modest savings became worthless overnight. Many Jews worked in finance, and small investors blamed them for what happened to their money and for the evils of capitalism.

The anti-semitic parliamentarian Georg von Schönerer said the Jews had caused the stock market crash, and that Austria should unite with Protestant Germany. It was he who also suggested replacing the benevolent greeting *Grüss Got* with *Heil*, and came up with the idea of "punishment camps". The mood towards Jews was changing. Rather than the Christ killers of the past, they were now portrayed as corrupt speculators and cynical cosmopolitan businessmen. Newspapers published anti-semitic cartoons of men with hooked noses and fleshy lips, clasping fat cigars. In July, a cholera epidemic swept through Vienna and kept away many foreigners planning to visit.

And yet Jews like Siegmund were migrating to

Vienna in such numbers that by 1914 they accounted for 10 percent of the population. Like him, most of the working poor were apprenticed to master craftsmen. His first boss was a Christian who drank, and expected Siegmund to help his wife in the kitchen and babysit his small children. The next boss was a kinder man, a Jew. Siegmund must have mentioned the men's religions, or how else would this be known? He was taught how to upholster furniture and hang wallpaper, but he also had to load carpets and mattresses onto a hand-drawn carriage, and haul them back to the workshop where they were thrashed or refilled with horsehair. The horse-drawn carriages and the wicked Föhn wind from the Hungarian plains created lots of dirt, and filled Siegmund's lungs with it. He was strong and stocky, but his health was always to be fragile.

How did my great-grandfather land so firmly on his feet? In her memoirs his daughter Emma writes that he was miserable. Winters in Vienna can be bitterly cold, and he was so poor he had to share a coat with another apprentice. The second-hand boots he bought with his first wages pinched his feet; and he was conned by a crooked salesman into buying torn trousers. He worked so hard he had little time to see his brother or his favourite sister who was employed as a cook.

Siegmund told these stories to entertain, but they upset a young Emma and no doubt sowed the seeds of her socialist convictions. Later, she notes with relief, he ordered custom-made suits from the elegant Rothberger department store in the city centre. Siegmund enjoyed material comfort, partly no doubt for the awareness it gave him of his improved social status. He must have been proud to have come so far.

In 2017, the Jewish museum in Vienna held an exhibition on the subject of Jewish department stores. Until that day, I had searched in vain for references to Rothberger's. Now I learned that Jacob Rothberger came in for particular vicious anti-semitic opprobrium because his handsome store was across from St Stephen's Cathedral. Among anti-semitic myths was that of "department store Jews" who tricked their mainly female customers into buying shoddy goods and were destroying the "small" retailers. Rothberger died in the 1890s, but his sons had to sell the business in 1938 to pay the hefty levies that Nazi "Aryanisation" required. The store was burnt down in 1945.

Siegmund's first happiness came when he joined the Austro-Hungarian army, the vast, ramshackle institution that embodied unity in a vast land fragmented by conflicting cultures, languages, religions and traditions. Arthur Schnitzler's novella *Lieutenant Gustl* says it all in one long monologue. But for 19-year-old Siegmund, this was the first time he had not felt looked down upon for being poor or for being a Jew. He served ten years and three months in the Rifle Regiment, doing mostly clerical work and leaving with the rank of *Unteroffizier* (non-commissioned officer).

Until his dying day, Siegmund loved and respected the tall, blue-eyed Habsburg emperor Franz Joseph with the mutton-chop whiskers, and identified closely with his private joys and sorrows. His long years in the army gave Siegmund self-respect and self-confidence, as well as an education, and an unwavering commitment to helping "the little man", the humble worker and underdog. Emma recorded that he reported on a soldier for making fun of an Orthodox Jewish conscript at prayer.

By then, Siegmund's butcher brother had opened a bar in Vienna's 17th district of Hernals. He helped Siegmund rent a small bar in the first district's Wipplingerstrasse where he would soon be selling schnapps, an alcohol served neat or flavoured with herbs or fruit. This was called a *Brantweinschanks*, Brant meaning spirits. By law such establishments weren't allowed to install stools or chairs, in the hope of ensuring sobriety. Jews were ubiquitous in the liquor trade because the profits were good, and the work less onerous than hauling carpets and mattresses or other physical jobs.

Of medium height, with thick brown hair and a glossy moustache, Siegmund was now in his mid-twenties, and like many Jews he turned to a matchmaker because he wanted to marry a Moravian Jewish girl. An extrovert with a warm impulsive nature, he was looking forward to starting his own family. There was a grocery store owner in Brno by the name of Benedikt Haas, a pious man who spent a great deal of time at synagogue while his wife ran the shop, and their daughter Josefine was good-looking. She had a slight limp but was well educated, and having reached the ripe age of 24, was growing anxious about her prospects.

Dressed in his only suit, Siegmund closed the bar for the day and took the train to Brno. This was 1888, the year the virulently anti-semitic Schönerer and his henchmen burst into the largely Jewish-run newspaper offices of the *Neues Wiener Tagblatt*, and beat up journalists for reporting on the death of German Emperor Wilhelm I on the day before he actually died. They claimed this had been a deliberate insult to German honour. But Siegmund's mind was on more sentimental matters. He found the regal Josefine gratifyingly pleasant to look at. Her first impressions of the man with the deep-set brown eyes and strong hands were mixed. She was worried that his trade might be rowdy, and he himself appeared unpolished.

After a chaperoned stroll through Brno, and coffee and cakes, her parents took Josefine aside and asked if she had made up her mind. She hesitated.

"Could we meet again?" she asked. "No," they replied, "the poor man can't be expected to close shop again. And the way he looks now he'll look next time around."

So Josefine agreed to the match and a satisfied Siegmund returned to Vienna. When he came to meet his fiancée a second time, bringing a gift of a pin-cushion he had crafted out of silk and wood, they fixed their wedding date.

-5-

1890s: A golden age of security

A photograph of my great-great-grandmother Eva shows her with a dark braid crowning her head, hair strands interlocked like a loaf of Challah bread. This kind of hairpiece was much in vogue, perhaps in imitation of Empress Elisabeth, Franz Joseph's beautiful wife. She wears a chain around her neck, a brooch at her lace collar, and ornate, salamander-shaped earrings. The braid is the pièce de résistance, and the occasion a significant one, perhaps her daughter Josefine's wedding.

Crowning glory: my great-great-grandmother's imposing hairpiece

Three of Siegmund's sisters accompanied him to Brno on the big day. His first destination was the office where he was to sign the marriage contract, the *ketubah*.

Then everyone went to the dressmaker for the last fitting of the wedding dress and this is when Josefine overheard Siegmund say in the next room: "The money for the dowry I have also seen." She felt a stab of pain, having read about love in the romantic novels of authors like E Marlitt and Wilhelmine Heimburg. This wasn't quite what she had expected.

But the day was splendid, and the spring weather mild. Rabbi Baruch Placek, who had known Josefine since childhood, consecrated the wedding at Brno's largest temple. Moravia's last chief rabbi, Placek was a considerable figure, an amateur ornithologist and botanist and a close friend of Gregor Mendel, the father of genetics. He mentioned the bride's beauty. Family and friends then enjoyed a lavish spread of chopped liver, *kreplach, kugel*, jellied carp and many types of breads and cakes. When evening drew near, Josefine asked Siegmund if she could stay one more night in her parents' home. She wept at the thought of leaving them. He agreed and she joined him in Vienna the following day.

When she had had time to settle in, Siegmund brought his bride to tea with his redoubtable sisters. They wanted to examine Josefine more closely, and the one thing they all agreed on was that she was too thin.

"Do you eat *Beuschel*?" one asked, referring to the Viennese dish of veal lungs in sweet and sour sauce.

"I don't really care for it."

"What about fillet steak in sour cream sauce?"

"I've never tried it."

"And cheese strudel?"

"I don't much care for it," Josefine replied, never having eaten it.

"For God's sake, what *do* you care for?" cried the greediest sister, Tini, whose proud ambition was to taste everything before she died.

Bruno was born in early February 1889, less than nine months after his parents had spent their first night together. Josefine explained this premature birth as having been caused by deep shock at hearing the news of Prince Rudolph's suicide at the imperial hunting lodge in Mayerling. "I felt such deep sympathy for the Royal house," she said.

The prince had had a stormy relationship with his father Franz Joseph who had excluded him from state affairs. Rudolph believed in a democratic and multi-ethnic monarchy, and saw the western democracies, and not Germany, as his country's natural allies. His death was ascribed to an aneurism, but newspapers soon revealed the scandal of a double suicide with his young mistress. Murder was one of the many rumours that made the rounds.

Because baby Bruno was underweight, his circumcision was postponed until he reached three kilos on the scales. The ritual was then performed in the tiny apartment. "They did not stint on prayers," Josefine later wrote her son in a long, nostalgic letter, which I read in Bus's English translation. "You teethed, walked and spoke at the right time," she wrote, "nothing very remarkable, but first-time parents who watch these early stages in their child's life are convinced that the experience is exclusive to them." In the evening when they changed the baby's nappies, the sight of the little wounded penis made Siegmund faint flat out onto the bed.

Newlyweds: Siegmund wore his best suit and allowed his hairdresser to be creative

In January that same year, the Social

Democratic Workers' Party was founded under the leadership of Victor Adler, a doctor from a Jewish family in Prague who had left the German nationalist movement because of its anti-semitism. It was also the year parliamentary representative Karl Lüger spoke in defence of the "little man", the artisan supposedly exploited by ruthless Jewish bosses.

For Stefan Zweig, this was the beginning of the "Golden Age of Security", Austria-Hungary's long period of stability and peace up until the First World War. Like many, Siegmund was optimistic about the future. Despite sometimes venemous anti-semitism, the world had greatly improved for Jews, and Vienna offered exciting opportunities for men like him. He moved to a larger apartment in the Brigittenau, the 20th Bezirk, a predominantly Jewish working-class district between the Danube and the Danube canal, next to Leopoldstadt.

On the first of May 1890, the first ever Europe-wide May Day parade took place along the Prater Avenue in a seemingly endless procession of men, women and children demanding universal voting rights, social welfare and eight- instead of ten- or eleven-hour working days. Franz Joseph had been ready to call in the troops, and shopkeepers had slammed down their blinds, but there was no violence. What did Siegmund and Josefine do? Did they keep the bar open? Were their hearts with the marchers? Were they concerned that the workers might riot and smash windows?

The family's first home was in one of those enormous Viennese apartment blocks with thick-walled archway and inner courtyard, where nothing is revealed to the outside world. They had a ground-floor room and kitchen, while the schnapps bar was at the back of the courtyard. Soon they rented the floor above for their expanding family and two live-in maids. Babies arrived in quick succession, all of them born at home with the help of a midwife – Richard in 1891, Klara in 1892, Otto in 1894 at the start of the Dreyfus affair in France, and finally my grandmother Emma in 1895.

Nowadays the area in Brigittenau close to the Augarten Park where Siegmund and his young family lived is a mix of the middle classes and immigrants, couples jogging in the park or taking their children to its small outdoor pool, and women in headscarves chatting on benches under the dusty chestnut and elm trees. Three *Flakturm*, German anti-aircraft concrete towers spiked with steel armour, stand on three sides of the park as ugly reminders of the Second World War. They can't be removed without blowing up much of the garden and surrounding streets, so they stay, occasionally used for art events and film screenings.

It took Bob and me a long time to find the family home when we visited in the 1990s, as Wintergasse is now called Hartlgasse. We finally spotted a blue enamel plaque with the old name on it. Wintergasse had been almost entirely reduced to rubble after the Allied bombings of World War Two, its ruins rebuilt in the 1950s and 60s into four- to five-floor apartment buildings. We walked up and down, but it didn't remind Bob of the place he'd known as a boy. He thought a small, unadorned house near the Augarten end was probably his grandparents' house, their second home in the street.

The year Emma was born, 1895, Vienna elected Europe's first anti-semitic municipal government, after Karl Lüger's Christian-Social Party crushed the liberal majority. Two years later, the Emperor reluctantly ratified Lüger's nomination as mayor, a post he held until his death in 1910. By then, he had softened the tactical anti-semitism of his electoral years, and many remembered him as Vienna's best-ever mayor, a man of few principles yet who loved his city.

He ordered the building of a second aqueduct to bring more fresh water into Vienna, which still today has the best-tasting tap water anywhere. Hospitals went up, a vast old people's home, more schools, communal insurance companies and savings banks. Lüger ensured that the forests and meadows of the Vienna woods were protected from lumbering and property developers. He also brought in an era of anti-intellectualism, and of nostalgia for a Vienna of beer houses, wine gardens and *Gemütlichkeit*, in many ways the Vienna that is still sold to tourists today. As his municipal council sidekick Hermann Bielohlawek famously remarked, "When I see a book I want to puke" (or, in earthy Viennese dialect, *Wann in a Büachl siech, hab i's schon g'fressn*").

Her father had wished for a boy, Emma wrote, because he had wanted to offer four officers to the Empire. The public degradation of French army captain Alfred Dreyfus, a non-practising or assimilated Jew, must have distressed him, as it did Jews across Europe. In France's *Le Figaro* newspaper, Emile Zola wrote that the affair "has brought us back a thousand years." He spoke of a hideous poison intoxicating the French, "the furious hatred of the Jews...fed to the people every morning for years." It caused Viennese journalist Theodor Herzl, until then something of a socialite, to become a militant Zionist convinced that Europe's Jews would always risk persecution and that they had to create a Jewish state.

Sisters: Siegmund joked that Emma, right, had been swapped at birth for an Ashanti baby

Emma was so olive-skinned and frizzy-haired that Siegmund said she must have been exchanged at birth for an Ashanti Negro. He was referring to the West African village set up in Prater's zoological garden in the summer of 1896, one of the popular European touring exhibitions of "exotic" peoples that was the mass tourism of the day. The Viennese flocked to the Tiegarten park that summer to stare at the hundred or so West African Ashantis, and Siegmund and Josefine were certainly among the throngs.

The eccentric writer Peter Altenberg wrote whimsical sketches about the African visitors, and told his friend Arthur Schnitzler that he had fallen in love with an Ashanti girl he had spoken to, and given a gift of glass beads. His stories make uncomfortable reading today, but at least he recognised the Ashantis' humanity. The anti-semitic press likened them to Eastern Europe's Jews, inferior beings of the same ilk, and the liberal newspapers wrote about the relativism of cultural differences and the brotherhood of man.

Siegmund was making his way in the world. He probably read the *Neue Freie Presse*, for which Herzl wrote, but that paper never printed a word about the Zionist movement, not even mentioning the first World Zionist Congress in Basel in 1897. The paper's Jewish publisher Moritz Benedikt may have felt that Zionism threatened his Austrian-ness by positing Jews as different, just as the anti-semites did. Siegmund would not have been in the least bit interested anyway. Before long, he was named vice-president of the guild for publicans and liquor producers, and because he had charm and spoke fluently, he dealt with public officials when problems needed to be resolved.

-6-

1900s: Snapshots of Viennese childhoods

The word "Grandmother" was a remote concept to me. I rarely saw this grey-haired woman called Emma who lived in America, spoke broken English and hummed to herself, sometimes breaking into bars from a classical song. She wasn't cuddly. Bob never put an arm around her, and she never hugged him as you might expect of a mother who so rarely saw her son. She liked to sit at the piano and make us sing, and my sister Lucy says this perhaps contributed to her becoming a musician.

My grandmother Emma in her New Jersey kitchen

Emma had been many years dead when Bob handed me a printout of her memoirs translated into English by her nephew Bus. "You might be interested," he said neutrally. I read them quickly before putting them aside, but I have since read them again many times. She had written them for Bob, his brother John and her own three brothers, and Bob had kept the copy in German intended for him, single-spaced and typed on crinkly airmail paper. I found this among his papers when he died: another copy of the memoirs Emma wrote in her sixties in the New Jersey bungalow, where she lived alone when there was no one to help jog her memory.

"She wrote just as she spoke," Bus had written in the introduction to his translation. "The Flatter family spoke with a Viennese accent. They occasionally used Jewish expressions, although usually for fun. It was considered bad form among educated people to use Yiddish expressions, except for telling jokes."

So why did Emma decide to bring back those Vienna days, spanning her childhood in the late 19th- and early 20th-centuries, and ending after World War One when she and her siblings had "passed their last happy and harmless days in Vienna before the great catastrophe occurred"?

Emma's American home contained few ornaments: some paintings by Otto, and her piano with a vase that rarely held flowers because she didn't derive pleasure from such things. But although she didn't care for material comforts, she could recall every print on her parents' walls as though they were still in front of her, including the photograph of Siegmund in his Rifle Regiment uniform, with green feathers in his hat. She

Emma thought her father looked stylishly Italian

remembered the texture of the green felt curtains, their golden borders, the tick-tock of the mantelpiece clock, and the smoothness when she ran her hand over the huge Grecian vases.

She remembered the schnapps bar's customers, her nursery school, Christmas presents, the rides and shows in the Prater amusement park, and the theatrical show of Viennese funerals, which were much more spectacular than most. Did it make her feel less lonely to leave the featureless landscape of southern New Jersey and cast herself back to the summers of her childhood, when near home the Danube canal's grassy banks were like the countryside and the children went with the maid to gather wild flowers, and look at the boats carrying apples from Upper Austria, and the barges laden with timber and granite paving stones? Did she hope it could bring her touchy brothers back together? Or was it simply the pleasure of remembering?

Emma recalled a happy household. Although Josefine was strict, Siegmund was fun-loving and generous. After 1900, Mayor Karl Lüger decreed that Sundays were to be an obligatory day of rest, and Emma cast her mind back to those afternoons when Siegmund closed the bar and the family went to a meadow in the Krapfenwaldl for picnics of cold rice and raspberry juice, or rode up the Kahlenberg on the funicular with plunging views of Vienna at the top. They would meet relatives in the Prater always at the same coffee house, and eat salami and cheese and talk about family matters, while nearby an all-woman band dressed in white played waltzes.

At one point, the Flatters ran two bars, the main one in Wintergasse and another in the Rauscherstrasse that leads to the fruit and vegetable Naschmarkt. In the early mornings, farmers on their way to the market tethered their horses outside, stamped across the sawdust-strewn floors and stood at the counter for buns and bread rolls, and to drink rum-laced tea or coffee.

Siegmund mixed his own schnapps in a back room, adding cumin and other herbs and spices to the spirits that were served in small shot glasses. As was the custom then, the bar also had a counter for coffee and tea, as well as raspberry and blackcurrant syrup and paraffin for lamps. Vienna's working classes liked to drink their tea with rum and often bought the two together.

The most exciting day of the month for the children was when spirits were delivered and a horse-drawn carriage drew up in front of the house. Siegmund always insisted on helping to unload the barrels, as he liked to demonstrate his physical strength as well as his democratic principles.

He stood in the street wearing his blue apron, watching the workmen roll the first barrel onto two posts attached to the cart's side. To prevent the barrel from thudding onto the cobblestones, Siegmund and the men leaned hard against it, lowering it slowly to the ground. "This always made mother very nervous," Emma wrote. "She couldn't bear to watch."

Most of Siegmund's customers were barely educated Czech and Galician Jews, many newly arrived in Vienna. Siegmund gave them tips and advice, and wrote letters and job applications for them. His busiest day was Saturday, pay day, when people were in a good mood. He was much liked for his easy and gregarious manner, and his fondness for a hearty joke, and the bar soon acted as a social club. He put cushions on the window seats so that his customers could sit.

Having witnessed the aftershocks of the stock exchange debacle, Siegmund did not trust banks. Every night, he would lock the day's takings into his bedroom strongbox. Yet he had a relaxed attitude towards money, and "an almost frivolous equanimity in the face of material loss," his son Richard wrote. Josefine, on the other hand, was more concerned with saving, and Siegmund sometimes caught her using a small watering can to dilute the schnapps.

Siegmund's working days were long, starting very early in the morning, and he suffered periodically from ill health when he coughed with a rasping sound, and had bouts of vertigo. On doctor's orders he would take the cure in Trieste or Karlsbad in Czechoslovakia, later named Karlovy Vary, one summer coming home with a hand-painted dolls' tea set for the girls, which he set out on a table next to their beds while they were asleep.

While he napped after lunch, Josefine would take over the bar for an hour. When it was time for him to wake, little Emma and Otto would race into the room and jump up and down on the bed, chattering and laughing. "Father would light a cigar," Emma remembered, "and we would fight to blow out the match." The smell of freshly ground coffee wafted up from the kitchen, an odour Emma would recall missing intensely when she started school.

Running the household was a duty her mother Josefine took seriously. Around her waist she wore a jangling set of keys to all the cupboards, so the maids always had to ask for fresh linen or food. Even when the children had left home, she liked to keep the keys close to her body. There would usually be ten to twelve people around the table at lunch, including a poor Jewish boy from the neighbourhood, and stray relatives or children they took in once in a while. On Friday, they would feed a beggar, serving him in the hall on the inside ledge of the windowsill.

The week's most important meal was Sunday

lunch. "Naturally there was a large roast and a cake. Since we didn't respect religious food restrictions, there was also pork on the table. Siegmund would joke, *Der Schweinebraten ist so gut, den soll man einen Goy garnicht essen lassen* (Roast pork is so good we shouldn't leave it to the Goys). Father sometimes brought back a large ham from Stalzer in the Hohen Markt, and this was sliced every night for supper until the bone was bare."

The household routine was typical of many lower middle-class Viennese families. Josefine shopped for the meat, fruit and vegetables, while the maids bought the staples like sugar and lentils that had to be sifted for pebbles. When buying a goose for special occasions, Josefine would go to a Jewish woman in Klosterneuburgerstrasse. Emma recalled the gamey smell of rendered goose fat settling unpleasantly on her chest, and the lurid scene that ensued.

"Negotiations took a long time before a goose was finally settled on and laid on the table. Now came the question, did this huge goose have a proportionately large liver? The goose woman would insert a large needle into the animal, and both women peered inside like doctors during an operation, and nodded." Christmas carp was bought live off river barges from Hungary docked near the Stefanie bridge on the Danube Canal, which the Germans were to blow up during their 1945 retreat. The carp were kept in the bathtub until killed with a wooden mallet.

Emma describes in great detail the refurbishment of the family home. The furnishings had been functional until then; the buying of furniture and ornaments was the expression of the family's improved circumstances and a significant moment in Siegmund's ascension into the middle classes. Necessity had given way to a little luxury. The Flatters wanted faux marble, faux wood and other faux status symbols, while at the same time in more progressive circles the modernist architect Adolf Loos was lambasting the parvenu's fondness for such things.

Otto was about ten at the time, and recalled his father asking an Italian decorator to paint a fresco on the parental bedroom's walls. One of Siegmund's friends had assured him that the painter's lineage could be traced back to the great Italian artist Tiepolo. The walls had to be scraped and primed, but as soon as painting began Otto raced in to have a look.

"The master on a step ladder would dip his brush into a small pot fixed to a string around his waist," he wrote. "Then without looking down he would stalk on stilts through the room like a Golem, avoiding the many pots and bags and the burning paraffin stove on the floor."

Otto visited the room again two days later, this time with Siegmund. "Along the ceiling's edges was painted a broad, richly fluted cornice as of stone, framing a bright blue sky dotted with silvery clouds. My father was taken aback and asked what was still to be done. The painter came down from his ladder, pointed at the sky and said: 'There will be *bambini* with wings in each corner with the flowers of spring, summer, autumn and winter, and it will be very nice.'"

Siegmund ventured he might feel giddy looking up at flying cherubs from his bed, and asked "How about painting flowers in each corner instead?"

"The man stood silent for a while as if waiting for inspiration, then shrugged. 'You, Herr von Flatter, are the boss. You decide,' he said with a sigh. When at last the work was done there were four fat vases in the four corners of the ceiling, foreshortened as if seen from below and crowned with flowers, and sitting on them and flapping around were many-coloured butterflies."

Otto couldn't understand why his mother complained for days that Siegmund was too soft with the people he hired. He himself thought the results were extraordinary, and that he too would one day become a painter.

-7-

1900s: Jew kids, out!

Emma's first experience of anti-semitism was memorable because of how Siegmund reacted to it. Their landlord, Herr Schmidt, was the Brigittenau photographer. Siegmund considered him a decent man, and felt sorry for him because his wife was mad and his son-in-law a drunkard. But his feelings changed the day Schmidt yelled "*Die Judenkinder raus!*" at the noisy Flatter children in the yard.

Siegmund was furious to hear his sons called "Jew kids", and fumed all day. He was much cooler thereafter with Herr Schmidt, and sent the children to play in the Augarten park instead. The yard where they had once uncovered Roman coins was now forbidden.

It was Herr Schmidt who took an atmospheric photograph I particularly like, maybe just before the incident. It is summer, and my sun-tanned great-aunt Klara is holding one end of a skipping rope while Emma loosely holds the other. Emma must be about seven. She is very dark and wild haired, almost African, and wears an extraordinarily melancholy expression under her large, round forehead.

The yard: Klara and Emma hold the skipping rope. This was before the landlord called them "Jew kids" and their father sent them to play in the Augarten park instead

As she wrote, Emma inevitably looked back at why so many Austrians had bottled up so much hatred for Jews. She wondered what clues had gone unnoticed. Siegmund, like many Jewish immigrants, could sense the anti-semitism around him, but hadn't let this dampen his enthusiasm for life. As vice-president of the Publicans' Guild, he interceded on at least one occasion with Vienna's Karl Lüger, and rehearsed his speech thoroughly because he was determined to make a good impression. Later, around 1908, he had wanted to open a cinema inside an abandoned restaurant, but was not granted permission and the licence went to a Catholic.

The ghetto in Leopoldstadt, the district south of Brigittenau, was abolished after the 1848 revolution, only half a century before Emma was born. Since then, Vienna's Jews had entered all the professions, particularly medicine and the law, which is where Siegmund had hoped to see his sons make distinguished careers. Most leading Viennese newspapers were owned by and largely staffed by

Jewish editors and journalists. How could one fear the anti-semites when so many Jews were visibly doing so well?

The Flatter family was what is referred to as "three-day Jews", those restricting their practice to the feasts of Rosh Hashanah, Yom Kippur and Passover. Emma believed that even this was for the benefit of Josefine's devout father Benedikt, who moved in with the family after he was widowed. He taught her to read Hebrew, as she was the most docile of the children, and the other four refused. She was also the only Flatter child to go to the Seitengen synagogue for religious instruction. Once in a while Benedikt took the blond Otto to synagogue, and gazing proudly down at him would say, "Look at the boy! Mark my words, the Jewish race is not dying out!"

My great-grandfather Siegmund the pub owner helped his customers write letters and deal with bureaucracy

"I have a somewhat faded memory of Jewish holidays," Emma wrote. I can imagine a quavering Benedikt reading outloud from the Haggadah during Seder, the meal at the start of Passover. "We all held a Haggadah, and the grownups wet their fingers in wine, we in lemonade. Father naturally took part although he didn't know anything about ritual ceremonies." On Yom Kippur, the Day of Atonement, "Father and mother went to the temple. After two hours, father gave mother a nod, at which she descended from the women's gallery. Together, they went off to Gilly's, a good restaurant in the Berggasse, leaving grandfather to his devotions."

But the Jewish feasts were not nearly as colourful to little Emma as were her daily trips to the Brigittenau church in May when the maid took her to admire the lavishly decorated altar to the Virgin Mary. Quite as spectacular was the Corpus Christi procession at the end of May or early June when the Flatter children would lean far out of their windows for a good view of the street below strewn with branches and leaves, and the parade of dressed-up children, incense-burning priests and devout followers. Corpus Christi was an occasion for Austrians to evoke the close connection between church and state.

Siegmund was proud of what he had achieved, but he never looked down on those less fortunate than he. He had three principles in life: behave kindly to simple folk, always have a full larder, and help family members in need. True to this last principle, Siegmund had founded a welfare club for relatives and friends, and once a year rented a room in a Stephaniestrasse hotel restaurant for a fund-raising party.

Despite having social aspirations for all three of his sons, only the middle one, Richard, turned out to be a scholar. Bruno, a spirited boy whose personality was akin to Siegmund's, drove his teachers to distraction, and Siegmund had to send him at 15 to a commercial college in Brno. Otto suffered desperately at school until he was he allowed to go to art school, when his future as a talented painter became clear.

Although he sometimes punished them, Siegmund was rather proud of the boys' rowdiness and enjoyed their company. He would wait for Josefine to be out of earshot to slip into the hand of studious Richard a silver coin in reward for his school results. "How I loved my father on such occasions, and how proud I was!" Richard wrote. "Not because of the money, but because he drew me into some sort of conspiracy and trusted me - just as one man trusts another."

Only Richard would realise his father's quintessentially Jewish dream of seeing his sons become doctors or lawyers. He studied law to please him, but his true passion was for the theatre, and Saturday and Sunday evenings from the age of 14 he could be found at the Burgtheater, the royal theatre on the Ring.

Bruno the most undisciplined of the boys

"You cannot imagine what it meant for me to stand there and watch characters like Lear, Macbeth and Othello commit their crimes and follies. During my first nights of *Othello* and *King Lear*, it was as if some cruel giant had torn my heart out from my chest, trampled on it, then scrubbed it with a rough brush and put it back again. I would go home mentally and physically exhausted, my heart brimming over with happiness."

Much as Emma loved her father, she still resented him all those years later for not keeping his promise to continue her education beyond the age of 14. She believed that had she not been hampered she would have gone to university, like Richard and studied medicine. This was the time when Vienna was renowned for its pioneering medical school, economists and art history theorists, many of them Jewish, although women among them were few.

"Mother found that the boys' education had cost enough money, and that I should learn a craft in case I didn't get married. With my olive skin, I was considered an ugly girl." She was sent to train with a milliner, and passed in secret the entrance examination to a teacher training college. Josefine did not object because the school was free. But being the only Jewish student made Emma uneasy. "Later, when I went to the municipal employment office to apply for a kindergarten teacher post, I was asked if I was a Jewess and was told unequivocally that I could not expect a position."

Photographs of Emma around that time reveal a slim girl with a small pointed chin, pretty even if she lacks her mother's haughty features. She believed she was the family's ugly duckling, and that no one ever listened to her. Yet her mother's dire predictions were proved wrong. A cousin from Brno came to ask Josefine for a favour; her son, Arthur Graumann, the apple of her eye, would be studying law at Vienna University. She was worried that he might be lonely, so might Josefine invite him over occasionally?

Arthur was an excellent musician, and when he turned up at the Wintergasse home, "soon all manner of sheet music was bought, and classical music entered the house." The Flatter brothers joined in, as all three played the violin, and seated beside him on the piano bench was Emma turning the pages. "When Arthur was coming, I would run all the way home from school, abandoning my friends, because I did not want to miss any of the music. It is no wonder, as our companionship coincided with my puberty, that I secretly adored him."

-8-

Poet and painter: two very different brothers

As she typed away in her living room, panes misting over in the New Jersey winter, Emma was evoking Vienna before the Anschluss when she still had a family around her. Now she was alone in America. Her three brothers were on another continent, her husband had left her, and her sons were far away, Bob in France and John in nearby New York but chillingly distant in his affections. Writing helped her recreate the days, however imperfect they may have been, when she was in her own country, speaking her own language, immersed in what was familiar.

Many years ago, Bob handed me his uncle Richard's memoirs. They were typed and held together by rusting paper binders, inside a cardboard folder marked *Lebensgeschichte* (biography). On the front page is Richard's London address in South Kensington, where he lived for a while in a small apartment in a red brick mansion. He starts his story by clearly stating his former social status. "Lawyer by profession, musician by inclination, anti-Nazi journalist, Shakespeare translator, theatrical producer, and playwright."

When he wrote it, he was lying in a hospital bed in London, a 54-year-old refugee with no money and no way of making a living. The war had just ended. "While I lay in hospital, hoping to get rid of recurrent attacks of fever, I had plenty of time to summon up remembrance of things past," he wrote, "and my life rolled behind my closed eyes like a film." His thoughts resembled "an old movie with blanks between the scenes, and long pauses during which nothing could be heard except for the humming noise of the running motor."

These memoirs were clearly written for publication, even if there were to be no takers. They are more about theatre, Shakespeare and language than family, or family in so far as it influenced his passion for Elizabethan verse. I was ten years old when Richard died at the age of 69, and we never met. I have photos from Vienna of a balding man with round glasses, dressed in a baggy suit, and I've seen sketches of him by his brother Otto, always posed in three-quarter profile to conceal his walleye.

Otto's memoirs came into my possession much later, after I had met Bob's cousin Peter, who was Otto's son. I hadn't known they existed until I saw them quoted in a British historian's article about exiled Jewish artists. I mentioned this to Peter, and soon the battered red binder was in my mailbox, posted from Peter's home in Sussex, England. Like Richard, Otto had written in English, his typed pages cut and pasted, sections crossed out, blue ink corrections in a forceful hand. Otto was 80 when he wrote them in 1974, looking back on a painter's career disrupted by the Second World War. Peter told me he had skimmed through, but had found nothing he was looking for. They were mine to keep.

"Late in 1934," Otto began, "an alien arrived in Dover. To the immigration officer's first question he replied in self-taught English. The officer smiled, looked at the alien's Austrian passport, and repeated his question in German. The alien was embarrassed and said to himself: 'Wait, Sir, you shall take me for an Englishman should we meet again in ten years' time!" Forty years later, he wrote, people still asked him where he came from.

A visit to Otto's studio: My sisters Diane and Tessa with the artist and our dad

I had first met Otto in Grilly, the village of my childhood in France, where he came to visit with his pianist wife Hilde, whose looks Bob had much admired as a child. "She was the first woman I fell in love with," he wrote, "for her beauty and also because she played the piano wonderfully." I saw Otto again later in London by which time he was widowed. He was old then, and like many old people didn't turn the lights on when darkness fell. Gloom descended on the kitchen and with it a certain sadness. He made a pot of strong English tea and we ate digestive biscuits.

My half-sisters were there, too, little French girls with chestnut curls, blue jeans and Breton sweaters. We visited his studio behind the house in London's St Johns Wood where Hilde's grand piano remained, and paintings hung everywhere on the walls or were stacked against them. The cottage and studio have long since been torn down. The low rent protected Otto from expulsion, and the depredations of the property developers were held at bay until he died.

Writing in English must have represented a challenge for both brothers, perhaps an act of

Richard was the literary brother

conquest mingled with post-war discomfort with the German language. Both used it very well, although their styles are completely dissimilar: Richard's wordy and lyrical, Otto's succinct and self-contained. They were born three years apart, but their temperaments were light years away, and the passage of time didn't change that.

Richard and Otto's differences are epitomised in the anecdotes each tells about early love, or sexual awakening in Otto's case. Otto mentions an early adult love affair; Richard remains frustratingly silent on the subject of adult romance, although he had the reputation in the family of being a lady's man. So I had little to work on, except for an insight into each brother's sentimental education. The object of Richard's childhood affection was a widowed washerwoman's daughter who lived in two rooms at the back of the family home's back yard. He was eight.

"She was no beauty," Richard writes of 13-year-old Fanny. "Her hands, it is true, were white and her fingers long and tapered. Her face was almost white, and her eyes a soft pale blue. I can still see her flaxen hair: it fell in waves and covered her back

- but this back was a hunchback." Richard would sit in her mother's tiny, steam-filled kitchen, from where he could see the bedroom with its two beds, and a picture of the Virgin Mary whose heart floated outside her body and was pierced by converging swords.

He would read aloud to Fanny from a book resting on the window-sill. "I don't think she paid much attention to what I read, but when I had finished she always said something nice, how beautiful the story was and how well I had read it, and that was bliss. From the kitchen, like a steady accompaniment, came the swishing sound of her mother's scrubbing brush. When I think of it even now my heart is filled with a deep feeling of peace."

On one occasion, Fanny spent two months in Istria on the Adriatic coast at a home for sick children run by the Vienna Council, returning with a small sun-baked die she had moulded out of red loam especially for Richard. "I loved that little die not only because she had made it for me, but also because it was tangible proof of the existence of southern sun and sea shores." But not long afterwards, Fanny was taken to hospital and did not return.

"I cannot remember how I learned of her death and what my reaction was. It seems I had developed my special ability to forget unhappy events. But I do remember that I kept that die for a year in my drawer until it was a shapeless piece of clay. When one day our maid threw out what she thought was dirt, I flew at her so violently that my mother had to intervene. When I was by myself again, I started to cry and I think it was only then that I realised what I had lost. My later love affairs were of a different nature and gave me more happiness, but never did I love with so unselfish a passion."

The five Flatter children: left to right my grandmother Emma, Richard, Otto, Klara and Bruno

Otto's recollection is less romantic. He recalled the day a girl walked into his father's bar. "She may have been about twelve, my age, and how poor she must have been for her face, her lips, were bare of colour, her hair unkempt, the patched light frock she wore had certainly not been made for her. Although it was late and cold outside, she wore no shoes. But her poverty did not oppress her, her bearing was proud and determined. A light bandage around her neck helped to straighten her back, to uplift her head. The bandage was not clean, but on her it looked like a precious necklace."

Another poor girl, among so many poor girls in early 1900s Vienna. Otto was standing idly behind the counter; the shop assistant asked the girl what she wanted. She looked at Otto fixedly. "I felt my blood reverse its course, my body trembled. She must have thought I was knowing, but I was deeply ashamed of still being a child." I like the Victorian "knowing" to say sexually experienced. "At last she turned her head to the assistant, and in a low, husky voice she asked for a paper bag of coffee. When she went to the door, she turned her pale face towards me, locked her eyes into mine, and with a jerk of the head ordered me to follow her."

Otto did not dare to venture outside. "Her boldness had struck my heart with enchantment and fear; I would not be able to speak to her, I would not know what to say, what to do, she would laugh with devilish laughter at my stupidity." He went slowly to the door, aware that he was too late. "I knew that I would long for the poor girl with the bandage around her neck, that she would beckon me and that my legs would be too slow to carry me to her."

What do these two anecdotes tell beyond Vienna's grinding poverty, children stunted in their growth, girls mature beyond their years, a whiff of child prostitution and consumptive death? Who knows what my great-uncles really felt. In the way they are told, the choices of words and subjects reveal a distinctive inner poetry: Richard's sentimental, nostalgic, Otto's more brutal, more direct, perhaps also foretelling some of his later passivity in the face of his friends' and family's distress.

-9-

1908: Liaisons and love affairs

The opportunity arose in 1908 for Siegmund to fulfil his long-held dream of becoming a home-owner, but two major impediments stood in his way. The first was that he had just spent most of his savings on redecorating the family home and renovating the bar. The second was that the house at number 5 Wintergasse, which came up for sale when its owner died, could not be sold to a Jew. But with Vienna's acute housing shortage, buying a home meant a step up in the world, as well as freedom from landlords and janitors.

"I remember father standing next to the cash register, rubbing his left eye with the palm of his hand, looking worried," Emma wrote. But after consulting his rich brother-in-law Ignatz, who firmly advised him against acquiring the house, Siegmund made up his mind and borrowed some money to do so.

The owner, a Catholic woman, had stipulated in her will that the house had to go to a Catholic buyer as it contained an altar brought out every Corpus Christi day to be blessed. Siegmund asked the artisan in the back yard of his apartment block if he would act as an interim buyer, promising him a studio at the back. But not having been able to visit before the sale, Siegmund had been characteristically over-optimistic, and the house turned out to be far smaller than he had hoped.

The artisan was not to get his studio, which may be why a guilty-feeling Siegmund asked him to design the new facade panelling with painted wood patterns. He had the kitchen tiled and a large ceramic-tiled stove installed, as well as the family's first bathroom. The bulky Biedermeier furniture was squeezed in. "With danger to life and limb," wrote Emma, "our dining room furniture was carried up the narrow stairs past Saint Michael in his niche in the stairway who looked on in silence."

The bar was on the ground floor on the street side, and the living room looked out onto the back. The boys slept there on the sofas, and the parents and the girls had bedrooms upstairs.

Arthur Graumann turned up at the Flatter home soon after the move, and made an excellent impression. He was short of stature, but his strikingly pale blue eyes crinkled at the corners when he smiled, and if Emma would later reproach him for using his charm too readily, it dazzled her then. The parents thoroughly approved of Arthur's excellent manners, and his Czech accent was the pleasant melody of their childhoods. He was soon visiting two or three times a week on the afternoons and evenings when he was free from his studies or from tutoring the sons of rich Jewish families.

The younger Flatters were delighted because he introduced chamber music into the home. They all practised music, but when Arthur arrived they started doing so together. Long abandoned by Klara, the piano was still regularly played by Emma in lonely solemnity, but now they bought sheet music, mostly violin sonatas with piano accompaniment, and set to work. Arthur was a fine pianist, Otto and Richard both handled the violin passably well and, after a while, Richard sang Schubert Lieder in his pleasant, soft voice, and soon more challenging work by Hugo Wolf.

Emma felt she was the family's Ugly Duckling, and would later read the story to her sons

"I also tried to sing," wrote Emma, "but secretly because I was shy of criticism." There was the added stigma that Siegmund disapproved of girls who took singing too seriously, as "Catholic girls go to nunneries and Jewish girls go on the stage", he said. He was referring disparagingly to some young women in Josefine's family who sang light music professionally. "So my singing remained a secret love."

Occasionally, Siegmund himself would come up from the pub and sit down to listen. "Now stop with all this Mozart tü-tü-tü," he'd interrupt, "and play me a waltz!" and the young men would strike up some three-four rhythm by Johann Strauss or Josef Lanner, to which he would tap the beat on the floorboards.

As the 13-year-old Emma sat at the piano turning the pages of a Mozart sonata for Arthur, she was in awe of this cousin who appeared so much more refined than her brothers. I find this scene of quiet complicity affecting because Emma must have felt that someone was paying attention to her, and also because my grandparents' courtship heralds my own existence. Over the next few years, Arthur urged her to read books and to go to concerts, and was altogether stimulating and attentive. Emma reminded him of his little sister Ilka.

The boisterous Bruno had long left the Wintergasse home. Having been expelled from the Florisdorf gymnasium for placing a lit cigarette between the gypsum lips of Demosthenes, charring the statue, Bruno was enrolled aged 15 at a textile school in Brno. The Czech town seemed the right choice, as Siegmund knew the place well and this was also one of the rare technical schools in the Austro-Hungarian Empire that allowed graduates to become one-year volunteers (*Einjährig Freiwillige*) in the Austro-Hungarian army. These were young men who enrolled at their own expense and were entitled to officer rank.

"It was not an easy decision," Josefine wrote in a letter to Bruno about his move to Moravia, "as the mere thought of the distance that was to separate us was painful." Everyone missed his high spirits, and the house suddenly seemed quiet and empty, even if his brothers had more room to themselves. To cheer everyone up, Josefine secretly arranged for Bruno to visit on All Saints Day. "When you walked into the room," she wrote, "there was a moment of silence, and then your siblings burst into tears of joy. I must admit that your father and I too had wet eyes."

Bruno's four-year studies were to be a heavy burden on the family budget. "Your father behaved like a wealthy man, even bringing presents to your landlady," Josefine wrote, "but we couldn't have managed financially to do the same for all five children. Mercifully, Richard cost us very little."

Like his cousin Arthur, Richard was to study law at Vienna University, having briefly considered medicine, but "I felt I should not be able to dissect corpses or, still less, cut into quick flesh." He pursued his passion for the theatre, his heart only half in his legal studies. But it was enough for Siegmund that Richard was going to be a lawyer, more than compensating for the fact that his poor eyesight had ruled out the army. "He who had passed his Matura with such ease could not become an officer!" Emma wrote ironically. "Mother cried, but she cried even more when Bruno had to join up when the First World War broke out."

Moments of complicity: Klara and Richard shared a passion for books and the theatre

Of the five Flatter children, the one whose temperament most resembled Siegmund's was the strong-willed Klara, an outspoken and relaxed girl with endearing dimples that framed her smile. He and she went together to concerts and the theatre. Richard was an enthusiast for John Galsworthy and G. B. Shaw, both very popular in Vienna. The two siblings read the same books, including Scandinavian authors like Strindberg and Ibsen. "I myself felt more attached to Otto," wrote Emma. "Together we attended Sunday afternoon concerts, and worked our way through the paintings in the Museum of Art and History, looking up the Old Masters in the Lübke-Semrau reference book when we got home."

In view of Otto's low school grades, there was only one way Siegmund could hope to see his youngest son become an officer: he would have to attend a technical training college like Bruno's. Josefine insisted he should learn a craft like gold- or locksmithing. Despite a valiant resistance, Otto spent four hateful years in a commercial school, before he finally sat the entrance examination to Vienna's Academy of Fine Arts. And to everyone's astonishment, he failed.

"I can't remember what he drew," his loyal sister Emma recorded, "but I am sure it was good enough. I suspect anti-semitism played its part because Jews were not willingly admitted to art schools." Siegmund sent him to a private art school on the Graben for a year, and the next time Otto passed with a drawing of the raising of Lazarus. Despite his expectations, the academy took some getting used to. The first time Otto entered its venerable halls, he was directed to a studio "with battered easels, stools, dusty busts, anatomical figures and charts that resembled a hospital ward where the inmates were not expected to recover."

In a decision that seemed terribly unjust, at least to Emma, Klara was allowed to continue school while Emma was not. "Mother had come to the conclusion that having always been a good pupil," she wrote bitterly, "I would get enough education on my own initiative." It was perhaps impossible for Siegmund and Josefine to imagine that one of their daughters could go to university and learn a profession. They had already come a long way.

-10-
1912: Choosing sides

Siegmund enjoyed a vigorous waltz and a low-brow play like a farce by the popular writer Ferdinand Raimund. But his children had far more sophisticated tastes, and were fascinated by everything going on around them. The year my grandparents met, 1908, Gustav Mahler was composing his heart-rending *The Song of the Earth* and Arnold Schönberg's *Five Orchestral Pieces* were causing furious debate. Klimt had finished painting his erotic *The Kiss*, and Egon Schiele was doing contorted self-portraits.

This was also the second time Adolf Hitler failed to pass the entrance examination to Vienna's Art Academy and was drifting about the city studying the demagogic skills of Mayor Karl Lüger whose oratory he admired. And Franz Joseph had just annexed the Balkan provinces of Bosnia and Herzegovina, precipitating the Bosnian crisis, itself foreshadowing the act that was to trigger World War One – the assassination in Sarajevo of crown prince Franz Ferdinand, the heir to the throne.

I have a large pencil portrait by Otto of Emma glumly wearing an unbecoming floppy rain hat, which she may have designed herself. She knew how to make hats, but was working as a governess. "Mother asked me to hand over my wages, as she had seen in her own home," she wrote, "but in view of our opulent household I refused, arguing that I paid for my French language and literature lessons." Later, Emma admitted that she had judged her mother too harshly and recognised her sharp mind and sense of social justice. Siegmund liked to call Josefine the *Allerweltverteidigerin* (the world's defence lawyer).

One summer, and without consulting her, Josefine organised a job for Emma at a poverty-stricken Jewish holiday camp near Brno. In hindsight, Emma understood that she was being kept away while her parents found suitors for Klara, unaware that she had fallen in love with Arthur's quiet brother Fritz in Brno.

Emma wearing one of the hats she designed

"She behaved rather badly to those young men," said Emma. She herself was growing comely, despite Josefine's dire predictions. "And it had also come *'nolens volens'* that young men showed an interest in me, equally in vain, as mother tried hard to keep me away from home. The penny dropped at last when father said to me, 'Be patient. All will change when Klara is married.'"

It was important to Siegmund that his children should make good marriages, so when Bruno fell in love with a pretty girl from a working-class home he couldn't hide his disapproval. His first-born had to do better than that. He attempted blackmail, the promise of a trip to Prague, the finest of uniforms for his one-year volunteership, all of which Bruno readily accepted while secretly carrying on with the affair. In the end, it was the girl who broke it off, no doubt because she realised that Bruno wasn't going to propose. He was heart-broken and went to work for a textile firm in the Sudetenland until the outbreak of the First World War.

Compared to provincial Brno, Arthur must have found Vienna incredibly exciting. He went to summer concerts under grandstands in the parks, discovered café life and the fresh Heuringen wines. Like most Moravian Jews, the Graumann family spoke German among themselves, and Czech with the maids and employees. Arthur had wanted to be an orchestra conductor, but knew he couldn't afford the early years of struggle, and had considered studying languages but was put off by linguistics. He decided to become a lawyer instead.

His father, the Moravian shoemaker Hermann Graumann, died in 1928 at the age of 74, but through the memoirs of my uncle John I have inherited a few words of his wisdom. A keen hiker, Hermann had solemnly told a little John, as he clutched the old man's hand during a hill walk, that "When you walk uphill, you must walk slowly with big steps. When you go downhill, you go slowly too but with many little steps." In one of those inter-generational transmissions, this advice comes quite naturally to my mind when I walk up or down slopes, along with the picture of the lavishly moustachioed great-grandparent I have seen in photographs.

In his 1908 novel *The Road into the Open* (*Der Weg ins Freie*), Arthur Schnitzler evokes how complex it was to be Viennese and a Jew. It came out the year my grandparents met, and Richard,

Arthur or Klara would certainly have read it. Schnitzler's Jewish characters – this is a roman à clef - react in different ways to anti-semitism, whether by ignoring it, fighting back, choosing piety or Zionism, or turning inwards.

My grandfather Arthur's mother was a proud pillar of the Brno synagogue, and had brought him up according to Jewish tradition, but in adulthood he resolutely turned his back on it. A sense of Jewish identity belonged to the past, he felt, and rabbis were irrelevant in today's world. Later when he spoke of Jews, he said 'them' rather than 'us'. I am sure Arthur like so many assimilated Jews considered with distaste the Jews arriving in Vienna from the ghettos of Hungary, Romania and Poland with their caftans, black hats, beards and sidelocks, affected perhaps, but feeling no sense of brotherhood.

Arthur chose the liberal cause and denied his roots, while Richard who was also a liberal felt proud of being a Jew. At that time, being a liberal meant advocating political equality, a political stance that was almost the sole preserve of Jews. I wonder if Arthur was among Vienna's assimilated Jews who realised that to anti-semites they were as Jewish as Leopoldstadt's caftan-wearing Orthodox Jews. I wonder if he read *The Road into the Open* in which someone accuses a character called Heinrich Bermann of having a persecution complex. That wasn't the problem, Bermann replies. The Jews had a security complex, not a persecution complex, and that one "lures you to

My grandfather Arthur did not feel loyal to his Jewish boyhood in Brno

destruction."

Schnitzler wrote in his memoirs that "For a Jew (in Vienna), it was not possible to ignore the fact that he was a Jew; nobody else was doing so; not the gentiles and even less the Jews. You had the choice of being counted as insensitive, obtrusive and fresh: or of being overwhelmed, shy and suffering from feelings of persecution." Did any members of my family have sympathy for Theodor Herzl's talk of emigration to Palestine? Probably not, as on the whole they would have seen moving to Palestine as an option for the persecuted Jews of Eastern Europe, not for them.

The Austro-Hungarian Empire's Jewish population in 1910 stood at almost five percent, and was concentrated in the largest cities: 8.7 percent in Vienna, 10 percent in Prague and 25 percent in Budapest, as compared with around five percent in Berlin. The same 1910 census showed that 60 percent of doctors in Vienna were Jewish, as were a majority of lawyers and journalists. In secondary schools and universities, almost half the students were Jewish. By 1923, when Eastern Europe's Jews were leaving the shtetls to pour into Vienna, the Jewish population reached 10 percent, double that of Berlin.

Unlike Arthur, Richard felt ideologically loyal to his Jewish past, which he likened to slavery. "Why should I be faithless to my forefathers who had faced persecution and martyrdom rather than relinquish their religion?" he wrote. "Who am I that I should feel entitled to regard their faith and loyalty as obsolete, as unnecessary, in fact as stupid?" The dandy writer Richard Beer-Hofmann, although older than Richard, was a relative and a friend, with whom Richard shared the conviction that there was such a thing as a Jewish identity, and that the Bible was its foundation.

According to my uncle John, Richard may one day have suggested to Arthur that he suffered from a lack of ethnic identification. In this imagined conversation, Richard would have replied, "I too am a Liberal but when the chips are down I am still a Jew. Where would you stand in a crisis if Jews were under threat? What would you do?"

But however ambivalent his feelings about being a Jew, my grandfather Arthur chose to court his Jewish cousin Emma. There is a park in Döbling, the steep and secluded Wertheimstein park with many winding steps, which I visited alone on a recent trip to Vienna. This is the park where they had secretly met in their early days of courtship for unobserved walks and talks. Emma's Pygmalion, Arthur, had become increasingly attached to her, still talking about music and books but also suggesting ways she might dress more becomingly.

On one such afternoon they were spotted by Richard strolling hand-in-hand, and he reported this to the parents. Even if they liked Arthur, Siegmund and Josefine did not trust any young male's intentions, and Emma was taken to the doctor, perhaps for a warning talk about the perils of sex. She was cautioned that Arthur would turn her head and then abandon her. He had an exalted career ahead of him, Siegmund told her, and a brandy bar's dirty little urchin would not be deemed a worthy companion.

Mama Graumann, as Emma called her future mother-in-law, was quite the opposite of the principled Josefine, and liked to hear the minutiae of her children's love lives. But she was unenthusiastic about her son's budding romance with a Viennese cousin who came from far too modest a household for her liking.

Meanwhile, Klara had made it public that she was in love with Arthur's brother Fritz, that they planned to marry, and that was that. Siegmund, whose health was deteriorating rapidly, was adamant that his eldest daughter should marry first, and Emma just had to wait while the dowry of bed linen, crockery, cutlery and other household necessities was assembled. This, too, was not up for discussion.

-11-

1910s: Paradise Lost

Lomnice was Siegmund's paradise lost. He took his children there to visit remaining relatives like the retired cellist who had played with the top orchestras of Europe and now lived with his sister in what had been Siegmund's childhood home. The Jewish population was dwindling but had far from disappeared.

"I ventured full of curiosity into the abandoned synagogue," Emma recalled, "and found a prayer book, the altar for the Torah, and an old harmonium that squeaked abominably when played." Otto later painted a picture of that synagogue, and the work now belongs to a museum in Brno.

Siegmund was thrilled to see his children adopt his childhood home, as this must also have offered some reconciliation with his tragic youth. It took almost a full day to get there, although Lomnice is only 170 km from Vienna, but the trouble was well worth it. After Siegmund died, the bucolic landscape, the streams, the woods and the invigorating smell of the country air reminded the Flatter children of him.

When his children were grown up, Siegmund

organised a memorable Lomnice get-together with the Graumanns. The Graumanns knew Lomnice's pinewood countryside, as they hiked often in its hills. They lived in nearby Brno, where Arthur's father worked as a shoemaker. His mother came from Boskovice, a small town north of Brno that is one of the oldest Jewish settlements in what is now Czechoslovakia.

Despite the family's relative poverty, the Graumann children were articulate and well spoken, with excellent manners and a good dress sense. Arthur's cherished sister Ilka, an elfish girl nicknamed the *Puppenfee* (fairy doll), seemed unbelievably elegant to the Flatter girls, whose wardrobe was mostly made up of plain pinafores in sturdy fabric. "I was most impressed by her light-heartedness," wrote Emma. "Next to her I was an awkward lump. She asked me what I thought of Arthur, but in those early days I didn't want to give myself away and restricted my praise."

The stay in the countryside was a great success. I suppose they went for swims in the river, walks in the fields and picnics in the woods, and felt they were lucky to have discovered each other. Klara and shy Fritz were secretly courting, Ilka was lively and amusing, and the youngest Graumann brother, Ferry, was still an adorable blond boy. They bought cherries and honey from the local farmers, and Otto sketched their likenesses with charcoal on paper. The four Graumann children could speak Czech and interpret for the Flatters, who discovered Lomnice in a fresh light.

My uncle John had a theory for why the family was called Graumann that explains why we are identified with that non-colour, grey, and its connotations of conservatism and sadness. The most obvious explanation is that Graumanns tended to go grey prematurely, but John wondered whether the greyness wasn't also an inward characteristic, an intangible something that travelled down generations. He saw it as a kind of wisdom, an avoidance of extremes. There was a character in German medieval puppet shows, John claimed, known as "der Graumann", a wise grey-bearded man who lived in the woods and pronounced a few pithy words at the conclusion of the story.

John was convinced of another thing, namely that my great-grandfather the shoemaker Hermann Graumann was only half Jewish. This meant a great deal to my grandfather Arthur and his youngest brother Ferry. In 1940, two years after the Germans had defeated Czechoslovakia, Ferry travelled to Slovakia and Moravia-Silesia, a German-speaking strip of Moravia, where he met relatives who confirmed this idea. I suppose they thought that this represented some kind of life insurance against the Nazis.

On this genealogical foray, Ferry found the records of Josef Graumann, the shoemaker's father. I have a remarkably good studio portrait of my great-great-grandfather, a stern-looking man with a chin-curtain beard, his eyes intelligent and wary. He was born in 1830 in Moravia-Silesia, now the easternmost part of the Czech Republic, then a possession of the Austro-Hungarian Empire, and a hotbed of progressive ideas.

The weavers of Silesia were among the first workers in central Europe to strike, and the poet Heinrich Heine wrote a famous revolutionary poem about them. Josef's grandsons believed he was a German liberal activist who had fled retribution after the failed liberal revolution of 1848. This usually meant a greatly extended military service.

Josef, left, and his splendidly moustachioed son Hermann

Jewish or not, Josef settled in a small town with the cumbersome name of Turciansky Svaty Mikulas in north-west Slovakia, and married a Jewish woman. Hermann was born in 1854, and was 12 when the end of the six-week-long Austro-Prussian war of 1866 ushered in 40 years of peace. The restive Hungarians were pacified a year later with a compromise settlement that established the Dual Monarchy of Austro-Hungary.

The Slovak village held no future for Josef's children, and like thousands of rural people, they headed for Vienna as soon as they had reached working age. Hermann was just 14 when his father accompanied him to the town of Zilina where he boarded a barge going down the river Vah to the Danube, and from there made his way alone to the capital to be apprenticed to a shoemaker. Each of the three brothers chose a different trade so that if one of these trades fell on hard times, the others could help out.

Hermann's training was followed by three years in the Hungarian Dragoons, a cavalry regiment that had fought in support of the Liberal cause.

Although he loathed the army, he was proud of having been with the Dragoons. He wore their flamboyant red and blue uniform and kept their crested helmet as a souvenir. He also held up his trousers the Hungarian way with suspenders at the back rather than a belt or braces, and gave his two youngest children Hungarian names - Ilona (Ilka) and Ferenc (Ferry). Hermann did not see the empire in the same uncritical light as Siegmund. For him, the Emperor was growing old and incompetent, and nationalities deserved greater independence.

If Hermann didn't feel particularly Jewish, his wife Charlotte more than made up for this. At the turn of the 19th century, her hometown of Boskovice had had a famous yeshiva and a centre for Talmudic studies where prominent rabbis taught, and she thoroughly enjoyed the social obligations that came with community membership. Her conversation was spiced with Yiddish words and expressions. When Hermann in Brno returned somewhat unsteadily from a game of Tarot at the local bar, she scolded him for his *Goyim naches*, or gentile's indulgences. He in turn liked to tease the rabbi for eating pork, which he did without shame at the local restaurant.

-12-

1914:Thunderbolts of war

Trudging through the mud of Poland or sheltering from cascading rocks in Italy, the six fighting men in my family were to sacrifice much of their youth to filth and lice, blisters and sores, and the stench of infection and death. Their patriotic fathers had never experienced battle, so it was left to their son to lose their innocence.

Franz Joseph's successor Archduke Franz Ferdinand and his wife Sophie were shot dead in Sarajevo on the sunny Sunday of June 28, 1914. That same morning, Emma, Arthur and a few friends had set out to scale the Hohe Wand's jagged rock-face outside Vienna. "We had to place our feet carefully, and we were merry and carefree," wrote Emma.

Otto the proud officer with his sisters Emma, left, and Klara

They basked all day in the sunshine on the green plateau at the top, returning in the early evening to catch the train back to the city. Something was wrong. People at the station were huddled together in small groups. When they head the news, "we realised this would mean war, since there was always unrest with the Serbs."

Austria-Hungary had long dithered over how to deal with Serbian nationalism. This time, they would deal a "knock-out" punch. On July 5, Germany agreed to support an Austrian military strike, which everyone assumed would be over in weeks. War was declared one month after that carefree summer day. Russia mobilised along its border with Austria and, one week later, 83-year-old Franz Joseph stood at his palace balcony before a cheering crowd, still a popular figure despite the rumblings of discontent across his vast empire. Only those close to him observed that he was deathly pale.

Otto and his comrades, Otto sitting second row, fourth from right

Nobody had wanted war, but once it was declared the atmosphere in Vienna was famously joyful: flags flying, church bells ringing, bands playing. Otto was in a giddy mood. He was young and he wanted to live intensely. "Jubilant crowds thronged the streets. I was excited, I jumped from a moving tram and the conductor shouted after me, 'Don't waste your life, we'll need it on the battlefield!'"

For once, the Viennese felt they were one nation united under their old and frail Emperor. Novelist Robert Musil wrote of "the ecstasy of altruism – this feeling of having, for the first time, something in common with one's fellow Germans." Freud said that for once he felt deeply Austrian and proudly saw off two of his sons who had signed up as volunteers. Even the pacifist Stefan Zweig admitted to having been affected by the rare sense of solidarity and fraternity he witnessed in Vienna.

My great-grandmother Josefine was stricken - she thought of her sons, of the deaths to come. When Bruno received his recruitment papers, she threatened to demonstrate in the streets alongside peace activist Bertha von Suttner. "She said 'I shall shout for all women to unite against the war,'"

Bruno was the first to be sent to the front

Emma recorded, "and father said, 'Bertha Suttner has said it already, and there will always be war, it's part of human nature.'" Baroness von Suttner was a well-known figure in Vienna, much admired by Stefan Zweig among others.

Bruno, a non-commissioned officer, was soon called up and came home dressed in his new grey-green uniform. "I shall never forget how smart you looked," Josefine later wrote. "You were like Mars, the god of war! You can imagine that I was not exactly thrilled to see you go off to war, but your father and I were staunch patriots, and we had to let our crown prince go."

Richard's poor eyesight meant he was unfit for service, but Otto came home from his physical checkup with a bunch of flowers in his hat. "There were more tears from Josefine," Emma noted. When he was called to the front, Otto said goodbye to their servant girl but couldn't face his parents. "She covered her face and cried, 'He will never come back', probably meaning to say it to herself. But I was young and proud of my physical powers, and saw myself moving into battle at the head of a platoon. A fire-breathing sergeant had moulded me into a mechanical object. I could stand immovably in rank and file, and execute the strangest jerks a split second after the ejaculation of some indistinguishable shouts. I was fit for war."

My grandfather Arthur was working as an articled clerk for a lawyer in Moravia. When, before the war, he had gone for the army recruitment medical examination, Emma wrote, "He drank black coffee all night, his heart was racing and he was declared unfit." When his case was reviewed six months after Austria's general mobilisation he was sent to Odrau, some 100 km from Brno, to serve with the Fifth Rifles.

According to his son John, Arthur's abhorrence of war was such that he deliberately kept his pistol unloaded. His work just behind the lines was mostly administrative, writing dispatches about the numbers of men killed, wounded or captured. What he saw was so ghastly he never talked about it again. John wrote: "An unidentifiable cause for despair of humanity stayed with him ever after. In his words, the crucial years of his life had been destroyed."

At first the Habsburg monarchy was fighting on two fronts – against Serbia from the Danube to southern Macedonia and against Russia in the Austrian province of Galicia. The aim of Austria's Chief of Staff Conrad von Hötzendorf was to crush Serbia swiftly and to whip around and attack Russia, but his offensive wasn't rapid enough and Austria suffered huge casualties. Seven-hundred and fifty thousand men died in the first six months, and the Russians were able to cross the Carpathian mountains into Slovakia. A third front opened when Italy declared war on May 23, 1915.

The worst time was experienced by Arthur's brother Fritz, Klara's *amour*, as an infantryman - he hadn't the *Matura* school-leaving diploma required for officer rank. Regiments on the Eastern Front were under constant fire, and the lice-infested men, feverish, dysentery growling in their bellies, were so exhausted after the forced marches that they dropped in the mud where they stopped and instantly fell asleep. Fritz went missing and might have died had it not been for his sister Ilka's fiancé who discovered the field hospital where he was lying shivering with typhus fever.

Edgar Osers, Ilka's fiancé, was an officer full of braggadocio who was convalescing with the Graumanns in Brno because his left hand had been smashed by a dum-dum bullet, although the cause of that wound was to remain a matter of family conjecture. The socially ambitious matriarch Lotte believed him to be a genuine "Herr Doktor", a misapprehension he chose not to dispel, and she encouraged his courtship of fairy-doll Ilka until she found out the truth.

When his hand healed, Edgar was transferred to a staff command and promoted to major. He located Fritz by searching through army files and, against regulations, intervened to have him spirited from his grubby sick bed. Lotte forgave Edgar for his earlier deception, and agreed to the marriage. The Flatter parents provided the dowry, a generous gesture that removed Lotte's objections to Arthur marrying Emma.

Stories of enemy soldiers fraternising on the Eastern Front have come to seem apocryphal, but Arthur said he was there on Christmas Day of 1914 when Austrian and Russian troops clambered out of their trenches, hugged and shared liquor until they were ordered to return or be shot.

The first half of Arthur's war was spent in Poland, followed by another year in the Alpine precipices where during quiet moments he studied Russian and Turkish and struck up friendships with other officers who jokingly called him *Grausam* (cruel). He told John of the bloody mutiny by Italian-speaking soldiers against the Austrian army, as they smashed army trucks yelling "Austria *maladetta*!"

Five of my seven great-uncles were on the Italian front to hold the mountain line into Austria. As a junior officer attached to an Alpine battalion of volunteers in the mountains of South Tyrol, Otto "sat in trenches for nearly three years, waiting for the next and maybe final shell, fighting against lice, fleas and rats, quarrelling with my comrades over trifles, competing in coarse language and manners."

His brother Bruno spent some time in Lucca, Tuscany, and traces of his whereabouts transpire in Josefine's long letter to him. He was a railway officer in Ujvidek, Serbia, later stationed in Macedonia and in the Carpathian mountains, where he was injured. His mother didn't know this, but Bruno had asked his Hungarian batman to shoot him in the calf. Mercifully for him, the shot left no burn marks around the wound, which could have led to a court martial.

He was sent to recover at a hospital in the Carpathian mountains, and from then on his future looked considerably brighter. He felt no shame about his act; his son Felix told me that Bruno "would show off his wound to us boys, by then no more than a dimple." Always a smooth operator, Bruno made his way into the Hungarian supply lines and sent suitcases home with grain stashed in the linings. Hungary didn't suffer the same food shortages as Austria, and my uncle John remembered finding rice in those suitcases years later.

Emperor Franz Joseph died on November 21, 1916, ending the 68-year reign of the man even the hostile Czechs fondly referred to as "Still Walking". The tenuous bonds that had held together his vast empire of people, many of whom didn't share a common language, snapped. The youngest of my family's soldiers, Arthur's brother Ferry, was sent to the Italian front in 1917. He had barely left childhood. The hideousness of war ate a chunk out of all their lives, changing them from fresh boys into scarred men.

Otto's memoirs are haunted by recollections of carnage. "The wounded crawl towards you, seeking help from the helpless. Sometimes for hours things as big as screaming railway engines are hurled from heaven spraying death and dirt. Your brain threatens to burst, your limbs are dead, you pray for the final blow. Then it is quiet again, your body trembles violently, you creep into your dugout beaten, and no one must see your defeat."

Otto remembered night watches in South Tyrol when "the hour before daybreak is the loneliest, the hardest to bear. There is usually an hour's silence before the night recedes and both sides wait for their relief. The sky changes to a misty purple, then to a band of silver slowly rising on the horizon. A cool breeze makes the living shiver, awakens the birds. They soon chirp and twitter their song of life unending. And then the sun reveals the prison and its huge place of execution."

A drawing by Otto on the wall

It was the Eastern Front's Brusilov Offensive by Russian troops from June to September 1916 that is said to have put an end to the Austro-Hungarian army's will to fight, a major attack striking simultaneously at different points and taking prisoners by the tens of thousands. German soldiers had little respect for their peers in the Austro-Hungarian army, complaining that their country was "shackled to a corpse."

At the end of 1917, Otto took part in the routing of the Italians at Caporetto, in which 30,000 men died – 20,000 of them on the Austrian side. "I was among the hundreds of thousands," he wrote, "who, encircling the plain of northern Italy, were waiting for the blow that would open the gates and help sweep us from the hardy Alpine mountains into the fertile sunny land of Italy." By the time he wrote this he was an old man and had just read Cyril Fall's *Battle of Caporetto*, which drew him vividly back to the Battle of Monte Grappa.

"The place name Enego recalled the spotter planes that followed our troops, the precise and unrelenting Italian artillery fire from newly arrived British guns, the rows and rows of dead soldiers I saw when I stepped aside into a forest clearing. And then, when the winter set in, how we froze in our thin and torn uniforms, camped under the eyes of the enemy without shelter on stony, partly snow-covered ground when food supplies were scant and our drink consisted of melted snow." They stormed Castle Gomberto, desperate to open the way to the south, only to find more mountain ranges barring their way.

He described a ravine in the western Tyrol where soldiers took shelter as "the most unholy place I ever saw. It seemed to have been hollowed out by giants to serve as an arena for brutal combat. The sun never reached it directly above the steep walls, but a small area of sky was visible and there was moisture everywhere. By day we hid behind boulders as there was no trench for unobservable communication, and only when the grey of daylight had turned into complete blackness could we move as far as the enemy searchlights would let us."

"From time to time at night the big guns poured out their fire and a tremendous thunder would growl and howl from mountain to mountain and echo from rock to rock. Then stones would rain down on us and the dust would blind us. It was the nearest to an inferno man could imagine." Otto knew how lucky he had been. He fell ill with typhus, but "I was never scratched by enemy metal, I never had to fight hand-to-hand, I was never forced to fire my gun at someone."

When he looked at the map in his book about Caporetto, what Otto saw were the "hundreds of thousands of graves of friend and foe scattered over the plains of northern Italy, men who did not know why they had to hate and kill each other...When one grows old and has seen earth's hunger for the living, has seen its cemeteries grow and grow, one is bound to think of death as a permanent state and life as an ephemeral reprieve." He was decorated for valour, but did not feel proud and never boasted about it.

During the war, Otto drew a chilling self-portrait in charcoal and chalk that shows a man pale and lined, eyes hollowed out with dread and exhaustion. When I visited a cemetery on the Somme in northern France, I found Germans, French and British soldiers buried together. My relatives had all fought on the "enemy' side, as far as the French and Belgian schoolbooks

Otto's self-portrait of dread and exhaustion

of my childhood were concerned, which made these communal graves deeply affecting, one-time enemies united in death and decomposition.

-13-

1917: A country of beggars

The surgeon who removed my great-grandfather's spleen in April 1916 was none other than Arthur Schnitzler's brother Julius, but the operation was not successful and he had only two more years to live. He was too weak to work and the pain made him irritable, so while Josefine nursed him, the sisters looked after the bar. The back cellar gathered cobwebs and dust because alcohol was unavailable and Siegmund was anyway too ill to mix the schnapps.

"There was a great shortage of fuel and many people used spirit burners to do their cooking," wrote Emma. "We kept the little alcohol we had for ourselves and used some for bartering for food." Food shortages in Vienna were even worse than in Berlin, and were probably the key reason for growing civilian rage against the war and the administration.

The atmosphere at home was leaden. When not confined to bed, Siegmund sat at the heavy dining room table poring over the newspapers and waiting for letters from his two sons at the front. Josefine waited wretchedly at his side, her arthritic hip giving her pain, and the sisters pined for their loved ones – the brothers Fritz and Arthur Graumann. "The girls spent the best years of their young lives in a state of depression," Josefine wrote, "and refused to have dresses made, although I had bought them beautiful fabrics."

They also developed a new line of business. A well-dressed man came to the bar looking for someone who could produce fake brandy and an aromatic tea essence. He had connections in the ministry of war, and officers in the field missed their schnapps. Josefine conducted the negotiations, and promised samples. "We bought essences, father advised from his sickbed, and the samples were deemed fine. Klara and I were glad to be occupied," Emma wrote.

The cognac, which they called Ambrosia, contained alcohol and fruit essences, and looked more than presentable with a raffia weave around the gold-topped bottles and a label depicting a fruit basket. When the manufacturers ran out of bottles, "we went to second-hand dealers looking for matching ones." They packed the schnapps into crates full of shavings, hammered in nails, and used a special tool for securing a steel belt around each box. Regular orders kept them very busy, and they invested the profits in war loans. "Father was happy at the thought of securing mother's future."

Raising rabbits with Emma, right, and Klara, third from right

The economic embargo by the Triple Alliance of Russia, France and Britain was affecting people's health and spirits. The wealthy still lived comfortably enough, but most Viennese went hungry, standing in line for hours on end for a stale loaf of bread or a few potatoes, wearing shoes made out of cardboard. An innocent cold could kill. People roamed the countryside carrying rucksacks full of jewellery to trade against flour or some fat.

"I myself," wrote Richard, "carried a big leather briefcase to the Law Courts where a black marketeer worked at the buffet. Many days he'd have nothing to sell, but sometimes I'd buy half a pound of rice, or a quarter pound of something said

to be butter." Although they hated the thought, the family ate horse meat. They also raised rabbits until a neighbour climbed their garden wall and stole them.

Josefine reminded Bruno in her letter to him that when he was in Ujvidek, Serbia, he met his convalescing father half way in Budapest and took him to see Belgrade, which

Siegmund wasn't as strong as he looked

made a deep impression on Siegmund. "How full of hope your father was of victory!" wrote Josefine, going so far as to decree that his daughters should wait until it ended to get married, "but I persuaded him to relent so as to put an end to their suffering." I have a photograph of Siegmund taken then, wearing one of those all-covering swimsuits, his face tanned but his legs white and vulnerable.

Emma sent a letter to Arthur in the trenches suggesting that if they got married he could request two weeks' leave. "One heard a lot about wartime marriages," she wrote. "Young women wanted to see their fiancés, and there was wedding leave, and besides all girls want to get married." Siegmund promptly received a letter asking for his youngest daughter's hand, and he consented. Fritz wrote asking for Klara's hand, but as a corporal he had to wait longer for leave. So although Siegmund had hoped to see his eldest daughter married first, Emma jumped the queue.

"Arthur came straight from the trenches, and his journey in an open lorry took longer than anticipated," wrote Emma. "He did not arrive on Friday before nightfall, which made us worry that we wouldn't have the wedding on Sunday, as the Jewish officials were not allowed to sign anything after nightfall because of Sabbath." But he made it, and my grandparents were married on November 25, 1917; she was 22 and Arthur 28.

Emma and Arthur posing as true Austrians

The ceremony took place in the enormous redbrick Rossauer barracks on the Danube canal. Emma and Klara wore black dresses, which was the custom, and fur-lined coats against the fierce cold. Siegmund was strong enough to act as his daughter's witness. Back at the Wintergasse home, his sister Tini who loved her brother and food with equal passion, had baked capons from Styria and the wine flowed freely despite wartime shortages.

"It was quite tumultuous," Emma recorded, "and I got very nice wedding gifts, and a large sum of money from uncle Ignatz that we later converted into a concert grand." Siegmund told Emma that he would have allowed her to study had he known she would marry such an educated man.

The young couple went on a week's honeymoon to Salzburg and then for a brief stay with Arthur's parents in Brno. "It was a short-lived happiness! When I returned from Brno I realised I had left my wedding ring at my in-laws, and I was very upset." Fritz was given leave three weeks later, but Siegmund was too weak by then to attend the wedding, and instead Bruno acted as Klara's witness. I have a comic sketch by Otto showing the couple standing under the traditional wedding canopy, the *chuppah*, the chanting rabbi's upraised arms having pierced through the top of its cloth covering.

The sisters went flat hunting. Klara found a pleasant apartment in Brigittenau's Greiseneckergasse, very close to the family home, and Emma set her sights on an old house in Döbling where Beethoven had written his Pastorale Symphony in the days when Döbling was still a village with vineyards, orchards and a meandering brook that inspired the symphony's slow movement. The ground-floor apartment to one side of the building was for rent.

The house was on Döblinger Hauptstrasse alongside the Wertheimstein park where Arthur and Emma used to meet secretly. Even if the apartment itself was dark and gloomy, the building had a magnificent old garden. Emma decided to rent it at once, so that Siegmund could move in and spend his last summer sitting outdoors among its flowery bushes, gravel paths and gazebos. I went looking for it on a recent trip to Vienna, but it is no longer there and tall apartment buildings now line the park.

This was the spring of 1918, and everyone was praying for the war to end. Karl I, who had succeeded Franz Joseph, had a secret plan to negotiate a separate peace with France, but it collapsed when made public. After his return to Vienna, weak from typhus, Otto was sent to recover at the military hospital where among the nurses were ladies-in-waiting of the new Emperor's mother. One of these was a young countess who heard that Otto played the violin and invited him and another officer - an amateur cellist - to play at the Augarten Palace. This modest 18th-century building in the Augarten Park was the grace-and-favour residence of the ruling monarch's closest relatives, and is where Karl I's mother lived.

Smartly dressed in his officer's dress uniform and having taken off his greatcoat, Otto was wondering what to do with his sword when a butler tactfully asked if he intended to remove it before entering the drawing room. There he recognised the nurses sitting around knitting socks for the soldiers. The Emperor's mother did not appear, but the two men tuned their instruments and tackled Haydn and Mozart with more gusto than finesse, after which they stayed for tea.

"The butler came in pushing a small trolley on which there was white bread, ham and sardines - food we ordinary people had not tasted for some years. We had little to talk about, and the atmosphere was not a cheerful one. We soldiers knew, probably better than the ladies, that the war was lost. The question was how was it going to end and what did the future have in store for us? Did the young women realise that their future was in jeopardy, their lives perhaps in danger?"

They returned the following week to play again

for the same audience of silent knitters, but this time they were interrupted by an elderly woman who burst into the room. Rioting masses were marching towards the city centre, and officers had joined the rabble, while the police were standing by doing nothing. "This report was followed by deathly silence; fear paralysed the gathering. I wanted to tell the disconsolate ladies that I was prepared to offer my services in their defence, but the words wouldn't come. My loyalties were divided. Was it not high time, after four years of fearful sacrifice, to acknowledge defeat?"

A servant came in to say that the gendarmerie was throwing a protective cordon around the Palace, followed by an aged officer who told the servant to close the shutters. "Turning towards us officers, he said coldly, 'I think you had better leave us now.' Annoyed at being dismissed in such a contemptuous manner, and reproaching myself for my lack of chivalry, I slipped out of the room and the house, keeping close to the shadowy parts of the pavement to avoid being seen in my dress uniform carrying that ridiculous violin case. But all that mattered now is that I had survived war's ordeal by fire; the future lay before me."

The following day, 'peace broke out', with famine and disease the new fearsome enemies. Otto never met the ladies-in-waiting again, but he heard they had survived. The population had no wish to seek revenge against members of the Imperial house.

Siegmund died in bed on September 3 in the house where Beethoven had composed his Pastorale Symphony, a few days before the Austrian army capitulated. "So he was spared the great sorrow of seeing Austria lose the war," wrote Emma who was pregnant with John.

An emaciated Siegmund didn't live to see the end of the First World War

Richard had spent the previous night in an adjoining room so as to be close by, and in the morning the newspaper reported a successful case he had pleaded, mentioning him by name. "I read the paragraph to my father," Richard wrote, "and he was very pleased and said to my mother, 'Richard will become a fine lawyer yet.' Those were the last words I heard him say. I was late and had to go."

He was in his office when he received a telephone call telling him to hasten to his father's bedside. "In the taxi, a stream of quick and lively melodies cascaded through my brain. It was always like that when I was deeply upset."

Everyone was standing around Siegmund's bed. "He could no longer talk. He made a sign to one of my sisters to stand nearer. Slowly his eyes moved from one to the other of his children. When he saw me, he lifted his hand as if suggesting a handshake. I put mine in his, and he turned on the pillow, placing both our hands under his right cheek – and thus, like a child clasping his mother's hand, he left us."

I have already referred to Richard's sentimentality. Someone slid a chair under him, and he sat there for a long time. When he slipped his hand from his dead father's clasp, he saw the red mark on it as an unspoken pact between them. "I thought I understood its meaning and I have tried to act upon it. Whenever I am at a crossroads, I look at the back of my right hand. It no longer shows the red seal, but the pact still stands."

Richard doesn't say, but it must have concerned values of decency and loyalty.

The strangest thing is that Siegmund's sister Tini died immediately after him, sealing her adoration forever. "Aunt Tini was often with us in the Beethoven house to visit her brother," Emma wrote, "and she was there for his last hours. As she was about to depart, she embraced Klara, moaned and fell to the floor. We lifted the heavy woman and put her in a chair. A doctor was summoned but could only confirm her death. So we had a corpse in each room." Josefine, who had always been a little jealous of Tini's influence, couldn't help but note sourly that Tini had succeeded in playing the one-upmanship game right to the end.

Bruno and Otto were both on compassionate leave at the war's end and thus not directly involved in the collapse of the fronts. Arthur was with them, but his Czech brothers Fritz and Ferry experienced the debacle, reaching their homes in a state of exhaustion after many days on foot.

The war had not yet ended when the Czechs announced they were joining the allies of the Triple Entente. The Czechoslovak Republic was declared on October 28, 1918, and trumpets sounded from the roof of Brno's Gothic town hall near the Graumann home. In his shop my great-grandfather Hermann put up a portrait of the new Czech president, Tomas Masaryk. Austria-Hungary was no more. Jews had long believed that their future lay in identifying with the dual monarchy and its emperor, but now they gladly withdrew from the German side of it.

Unlike in Vienna, where starvation and epidemics accounted for over a tenth of war-time deaths, people in Brno had not suffered seriously from hunger, even though most able-bodied men were fighting. Many people knew somebody in the countryside who could sell them butter, eggs and potatoes, or some meat. After his youngest son Ferry was called up, Hermann the shoemaker managed the shop on his own making military boots, because shoes for civilians were put on hold.

In the event, the Austro-Hungarian army briefly outlived the Empire, as the soldiers in Italy waited to hear from their commanders that the empire had ceased to exist before they laid down arms. Then they deserted en masse. The High Command signed an armistice on November 3, and Karl I stood down a week later, ending 640 years of Habsburg rule. The independent Republic of German-Austria was proclaimed the following day.

The temporary republic of Vienna and the Alpine lands had lost three quarters of its food supply. Territories were ceded to Italy, and what remained of the heart of the 600-year-old monarchy was divided into six areas. Poland on November 3 and the Hungarians on November 16 declared themselves nations.

Klara told her son Bus many stories about the war, mostly about all those young men sent to their slaughter. For years she was haunted by a song the new recruits used to sing as they marched past the family home. In Vienna, the empire's collapse led to anarchy, with the influenza epidemic cutting deadly swathes through an already weakened population. That autumn it killed the painter Egon Schiele and his wife, both in their twenties. With no coal and no gas, two million people were shivering in the capital of a decimated, shell-shocked country. The Viennese cut down trees in the Vienna woods for fuel.

The Allied Famine Relief programme's food distribution saved many Viennese from starvation that first winter. There was no government, no army command, and transport and supplies had ground to a halt. Veterans, along with unemployed men and women and revolutionaries, demonstrated in support of a new world order. Austria's first republic was being arduously formed into a coalition. The two leading parties, the Social-Democrats and the Christian-Socials, loathed each other over social and class divides.

The new nationalism was bad news for Vienna's Jews. The Jewish population of the Austro-Hungarian Empire had been a minority made up of people divided by politics, social class, cultural interests and religious commitment, but post-war prejudice tarred all Jews with the same brush. *Ostjuden*, Orthodox Jews fearing violence, were arriving en masse in Vienna. Anti-semites saw an invasion, the Zionists a justification for their goals, and assimilated Jews felt more uncomfortable than ever.

In December 1918, the premiere of Schnitzler's play *Professor Bernhardi* took place at the Volkstheater, having been banned six years before. The professor of the title, a liberal and ethical Jewish doctor who runs his own clinic, is pushed out of his job and put in jail for two months after anti-semitic manoeuvring by his colleagues. An ethical, compassionate, apolitical man, Bernhardi is the victim of cynical ambition and greed.

"Inflation made beggars of us all," wrote Richard. "Unemployment demoralised hundreds of thousands. What was left to us? Mountains and music, that was about all. And yet we muddled through."

Stefan Zweig in his autobiography describes a night at the opera with the audience in winter coats huddled together for warmth, the spectre-like musicians in tattered suits, pale from lack of food. Because of inflation, his theatre ticket would have cost a thick wad of bank notes, but the hall was full and the artists performed as though their lives depended on it. Meanwhile, my musical, culture-loving grandparents' married life was not getting off to a good start.

-14-

1919: The scars of war

The aftermath of the First World War in Vienna was a second war against hunger and disease

The First World War left emotional scars on all the men in my family who had fought in that hideous conflict. They had known the deadly Alpine terrain where the Austrians faced the Italian army, the trenches, the tunnels in the snow, the waiting, the detonations, the killed and the maimed, and were "painfully conscious of life's darkness."

The rooms in the Beethoven apartment Emma had rented as the couple's first home were damp and dark, reflecting the mood beyond its walls. This was March 1919, and Vienna's streets offered the grim spectacle of thousands of beggars, among them wounded and crippled soldiers in tattered uniforms shorn of badges and decorations, orphans and war widows, and the unemployed, including the now jobless civil servants who had flocked to the former capital hoping to find work in an already overstaffed civil service.

Weakened and vermin-infested soldiers were falling victim to typhus, which was threatening to reach epidemic proportions. The parks were littered with rubbish, the streets lined with refuse. That morning's wages were worthless by the end of the day. People were hungry and that hunger made them angry. The frequent demonstrations were desperate and violent.

As an apprentice lawyer for Vienna's provincial government, Arthur's job was to confiscate the property of those who couldn't pay their bills, a task that depressed him greatly. These were days when gangs of young people marauded through the countryside looking for food. When Emma felt the first birth pangs, she decided not to mention them to Arthur, as he was sitting his final exams for the bar.

"His irksome job had made him irritable," my uncle John records in his memoir. "Emma waited until Arthur had left the house, as she was expecting her sister Klara's visit. Then Klara took her to the hospital at the other end of Vienna where I was born."

Johannes Wilhelm (later Hans, then John) arrived on March 7, 1919. The same day, Arthur graduated as a fully-fledged lawyer. In September, the Treaty of Saint-Germain-en-Laye confirmed the country's new borders, and formally established the new Republic of Austria, mostly made up of the German-speaking parts of the former empire.

Arthur thought it was best to be Czech after the breakup of the Austro-Hungarian Empire

Vienna had once been the capital of an empire of 54 million people, and now it was a modest state of a little over six million. Austria had lost its coalfields to Poland, its heavy industries to Czechoslovakia, and its granaries to Hungary. As French prime minister Georges Clémenceau said after the carve-up, "What's left is Austria."

Germany and the other belligerent countries Austria and Hungary had tough war reparations imposed on them. Having stood briefly on the Allied side, the other new nations escaped war guilt and indemnities. While Prague could look quite cheerfully towards the future, Vienna, on the other hand, was the capital of a bankrupt country with a hefty bill in reparations, although in the end these were never paid.

Not only were the factories and granaries that had powered the empire now situated outside, but Austria was surrounded by new states with sealed borders. Its extensive rail network was truncated, and Vienna's businesses were constrained by customs barriers, passport controls and competing currencies.

It took a while to set up Austria's new government, during which time unemployment and inflation skyrocketed. The Flatters' nest egg of war bonds from the wartime liquor business was worthless, like that of many investors. In the midst of this misery foreign profiteers hoped for bargains on things of value. Stefan Zweig, temporarily settled in Salzburg, remembered British people on unemployment benefits ensconced in the luxurious Hotel de l'Europe. It wasn't until the League of Nations' 1922 loan to Austria that the Viennese began to be lifted out of poverty.

Arthur chose Czech rather than Austrian nationality, and baby John's religion was recorded as Catholic. Czechoslovakia's new democracy was powering ahead with the creation of a healthy industrial economy. Arthur's heart was in his hometown of Brno, where people had clear consciences because they had not wanted war, as he himself had never wanted it. His irrepressible brother-in-law Bruno was there working for a textile firm, and his other brother-in-law with the scarred hand was soon to be earning a good salary at an insurance company. His young brother Ferry was smartening up the Graumann's modest store into an exclusive, expensive shoe shop.

In their heyday, which was soon to come, Graumann shoes were for men and women with money to spend. The business leapt a long way from the small shop with the workshop-cellar near Brno's townhall. The fancy new shoes were crafted in exotic leathers some of which would be banned today, like snake, lizard, crocodile, toad, seal and antelope. Cordovan hide was a speciality, an expensive leather that has to be endlessly rubbed to attain a high gloss. A pair of Graumann shoes represented a worker's monthly wage. The Czech premier Milan Hodža bought Graumann shoes, as did Alexander Korda and Cecil B DeMille who had them sent to Hollywood.

Meanwhile in Vienna, Arthur's brother Fritz had reopened the two Flatter bars, but he didn't have his late father-in-law Siegmund's ebullient temperament and times were hard. Workers were not drowning their sorrows in schnapps, judging by the sorry state of the family business. Perhaps they were too poor, too demoralised, even for that. Richard blamed his brother-in-law Fritz for the bar's meagre takings, and Klara defended her husband against her once favourite brother. Loyalties had changed. The Flatter family had lost its moral compass with the death of the energetic Siegmund, just as Austria had lost its certainties when the Emperor died and the country was dismantled.

The brandy bar did not survive for long after the war

Despite these difficulties, Klara was more upbeat than Emma. In her top-floor apartment, the furniture was of pale oak and light poured in through the large windows, reflecting her sunnier disposition.

Among the books the literate Klara may have read at that time was Hugo Bettauer's 1922 bestseller *Die Stadt ohne Juden*, The City Without Jews, in which a fictional chancellor orders the expulsion of all Jews from Vienna. At first the Viennese are delighted, but soon theatres fold, department stores close, cafés disappear, the banking system collapses and the economy declines to such an extent that the crowds call for their return. The novel enraged anti-semites, and in 1925 Bettauer was shot by a fascist, dying of his wounds a few days later.

Austrians were reduced to living like beggars, Richard wrote of the post-war years, surviving on the charity of President Herbert Hoover's American Relief Administration and that of the Quakers. He told Fritz that he would never set foot in Czechoslovakia, that country of traitors. The Czechs, he said, had had nothing to complain about under the monarchy. They had had their own university in Prague, their own theatres and opera houses, and even Czech members of Parliament. What more could they have wanted? Didn't they already have all the freedom they needed? Why did they have to seek independence?

Josef Roth's celebrated novel of the dying empire *The Radetzky March* conveys nostalgia for the days when the Emperor was still a reassuring father figure, even if his house was crumbling around him. Roth, a Jew, saw the Austro-Hungarian monarchy as his fatherland. "It permitted me to be a patriot and a citizen of the world at the same time." Like Roth, Richard was to remain a monarchist, convinced that it was the dismantling of the empire while Germany remained whole that had opened the door to Hitler.

The Austrian constitution was ratified in 1920. Austria was now a federal republic of nine provinces, including the city of Vienna. Vienna was the country's capital, as well as a province in its own right, and its government was run by the

Social-Democrats. One in three Austrians lived in Rotes Wien, Red Vienna, now separated from the conservative agricultural provinces.

Like many Jews, Emma and Klara were keen supporters of the new Social-Democrat administration that was to introduce universal suffrage, and progressive policies in housing, health and social welfare. The municipality also eradicated endemic child tuberculosis by opening sanatoriums and health centres in the hills around Vienna. Chancellor Ignaz Seipel, a priest, negotiated the generous League of Nations loan, and in Vienna the socialists financed their social measures by raising many small direct taxes, as on cars, horses and dogs, and by placing enormous contracts.

Austrians had always been nature lovers, and socialist rambling associations ensured that cheap weekend train tickets allowed thousands of men and women to head for the hills or the mountains, in summer and winter, where they could stay overnight in inns or hostels for a schilling or two. The appreciation of Austria's natural beauty was promoted even among the poorest. The Flatters were avid hikers, going for long countryside rambles with friends, wearing nail-studded boots, and along the way buying bread, cheese and bacon at stalls, or mugs of fresh milk.

The routine of family life resumed. Every Sunday evening, the stately Josefine received her children for an early supper prepared by the cook. The food was sausages and talk concerned family matters; my grandfather Arthur tended to avoid these gatherings as he found his mother-in-law too irritating. Josefine's rheumatism had greatly reduced her mobility, and she now leaned heavily on a walking stick, spending much time in an armchair at the living room window looking out at

Richard's husky dog, Nanouk, in the yard.

Her sons' success was what kept her spirits up. Visits from Bruno the businessman who now sold specialist paints and lacquers in Czechoslovakia saw "the whole house jump to attention", Emma recalled. "Shoes went to the shoemaker, suits to the tailor, gloves to the cleaner, and the phone was in constant use. When he left, mother would say 'I am always pleased when Bruno visits, but I am so glad when he leaves.'"

Her artist sons, too, were objects of pride. When Otto exhibited a portrait at the Secession, the art movement headed by Gustav Klimt, she stood beside it throughout the opening "to hear what the critics had to say and to relate it proudly when she came home", Emma wrote.

Richard tried to keep his plans to himself because his mother's boasting embarrassed him. "But how delighted she was to attend the theatre for the opening of one of his plays, always with a ham roll in her handbag to ensure her bodily comfort," wrote Emma, who would be by her side. She was proudest of Richard because his name regularly appeared in the newspapers, which gave her wonderful opportunities to boast to her cronies when they met in a café for coffee and cake. "Ah, look at this!" she would exclaim in fake surprise. "They are again talking about my son Richard!" pushing the *Neue Freie Presse* into the other women's reluctant hands.

-15-

1920s: Finding their feet

This is when my uncle John's memoirs take over from Emma's as the most detailed source for my family narrative, because hers stop the year she married. My father told me how sad he felt when he looked at photographs of John as a boy because John seemed so vulnerable and serious behind his small, round glasses. Foreshadowed perhaps were his future tussles with sanity. This is why my father gave me John's memoirs; he himself found them too painful to read.

John's memoirs are a thorough and hefty book bound in brown cardboard, which he addressed to his three children near the end of his life, aged 57. They combine chunks of history, chunks of memories and his interpretations of both, like views into his soul. This is probably why my cousins were reluctant to read them, because they didn't want to see into those depths.

I had mentioned them in Cardiff to John's cousin Bus, who became quite irritable and said that they were full of mistakes. I don't think that's true, but they probably were gruelling reading because they talk about Bus and his parents. So they came to me like hot embers, not neutral but still radiating John's complicated and candid personality. But I had the advantage that I wasn't reading them through the lens of those who had loved him; I didn't know him well enough for that. They couldn't hurt me in the same way.

At the age of 29, Arthur had fathered the first of his two sons but was no longer the confident young man he had been before the war. Emma and he decided to set up a law practice in Vöslau, a pretty town south of Vienna where noblemen once hunted. My grandparents had no connections there, and to build up a clientele the intellectual Arthur should have drunk beer with the villagers, and quiet Emma should have made friends and boasted of her husband's legal talents. But instead they went for long hikes, played the piano and acquired a goat that Emma milked in the kitchen, which the locals found inappropriate behaviour for a city woman.

Baby John's early days in Vienna

They stuck it out until they had spent their savings and had to pawn the furniture. The brilliant eldest Graumann son wasn't living up to anyone's expectations, particularly not his own, and felt so humiliated that he had a breakdown. "What had become of my father, admired for his erudition, social talents and charm?" wrote John. "Great things had been expected of him, but he had failed on the first occasion to prove himself."

In a dramatic decision, Arthur returned to Brno alone, while Emma and John moved in with her mother Josefine in Vienna. Arthur wrote regularly, but Richard was cross with the Czechs and crosser still with Arthur for shirking his responsibilities.

Rich uncle Ignatz lent Emma the ground floor of a coach house he owned near his palatial residence outside Vienna's inner ring, where she set up a leather hat workshop with a cousin. She was showing considerable pluck, and her reluctant years as a milliner's apprentice had not been wasted after all. Every morning, she took the tram from Brigittenau into the centre and returned late in the evening. Her mother and sister looked after John until Klara's own son Ernest, or Bus, was born nine months later and she pushed them both around in a pram designed for twins.

Those must have been desperately worrying times for Emma, left on her own with an infant, but after a few months Arthur resumed family life. John believes his father had looked into work opportunities in Brno where President Tomas Mazaryk was building a forward-looking democracy. In Vienna, he found a job with the newly formed Anglo-Hungarian Bank, and uncle Ignatz lent the couple a small apartment above the hat shop, where Emma was now dyeing leather jackets since hats had gone out of vogue. It had originally been a hayloft, and Edgar, Arthur's brother-in-law in Brno, lent some money for its refurbishment.

I don't know if this was common at the time, but Emma shared a bedroom with John, while Arthur filled his own with books. It may have been the best way she found of keeping John from crying at night and waking Arthur. John was difficult. Battles over food could reach epic proportions, with Emma no doubt concerned that John might starve to death.

When she could take it no longer, Emma would take John over to Klara. "Her friendly apartment seemed so bright and cheerful, and her food so good, that I returned much restored," John wrote. "As I ate poorly while Bus prospered, we were mistaken for twins, much to Klara's amusement. Klara shared her maternal favours so evenly that I believed she was my mother and Bus my brother." This feeling of alienation from Emma was to stay with John.

Bus with his mother, Klara, a far more maternal woman than her sister Emma

Otto meanwhile had left the Art Academy and was leading the artist's life. He wore a smock and grew his hair. "If I was poor I was not alone, we were all poor. We had all been helplessly watching our means running out like sand in an hour glass." He didn't have many commissions, except through his brother Bruno, and spent a great deal of time in cafés drinking coffee and discussing art, very much part of that world Friedrich Torberg describes in his iconic *Tante Jolesch or the Decline of the West in Anecdotes* that is a homage to the mostly Jewish intellectuals, chess players, eccentrics, wits, geniuses, poets and *schnorrers* (free-loaders) who saw the cafés as their spiritual homes.

Emma no longer trusted Arthur as she once had. To compound her concerns, all of a sudden he quit his job at the bank in anticipation of what he said would be a huge scandal. "What had been patched up erupted again like a volcano," wrote John. "My father said he had to resign and find another job, and my mother took this as sheer fantasy." But Arthur was right; the bank collapsed spectacularly in a widely reported case of fraud and currency speculation, "which helped my father regain some respect."

Otto's portrait of John, a solemn child with a passion for maths and geography

John was aware he was a difficult child, and knew that his distress and lack of appetite caused general concern. Perhaps he acted as a lightning rod for his parents' insecurities, and those of the world around him. Arthur would occasionally express faith in him, "but my mother would at best heave a sigh and say, 'Perhaps he will be human some day.'" He went briefly to a Catholic nursery school, but the children scared him and he cried continuously until Emma was called to take him away. She was deeply offended when a nun said that John was like the child of aged parents.

With Arthur unemployed, Emma combed through the small ads in the newspapers and found a job that seemed tailor-made for him. Solvay was a huge chemicals company founded by the Belgian industrialist Ernest Solvay; he had developed the ammonia-soda process for making the soda ash used in the production of glass, detergents and chemicals, as well as for cleaning metals and glass. It had factories across the world, and its central European headquarters were in Vienna. Political and legal conditions in the former empire having been completely transformed, Solvay needed an international lawyer to create new structures. Arthur was hired in 1923, and the new job would herald years of financial security, professional contentment and better companionship between Emma and Arthur.

John kept a wary distance from his father, seeing him as a stranger. But on his first day at elementary school, Arthur took time off from his new job. "He took me by the hand to meet my teacher," John wrote. "He said his father had done this for him, and so perhaps had all fathers before him, because what I would learn at school would be of lasting importance in my life."

Bob, the sunshine baby

Arthur visited the school again on November 18, 1925. There was a knock on the classroom door, and he walked in. He shook the teacher's hand and they exchanged a few words. The teacher smiled and told John he could go. "My father told me I had a baby brother to love and be loved by, and we were on our way to see him at the hospital. At last I understood that it was good to be part of a family and that one could feel proud of the fact." My father was so beautiful and smiley that Emma said he was like the sunshine and that he brought light back into her life.

-16-

1925: Red Vienna, my father's birthplace

The year Bob was born, Vienna's Austro-Marxist Social-Democrat municipal government was known as a model of the soft revolution, resolutely opposed to violence, and most intellectuals and many Jews supported it. Even if they talked disparagingly of "*Bankjuden, Börsenjuden*", the Social-Democrats were not anti-semitic, or at least considerably less so than the right-wing parties. They were anti-clerical and angry that the war had ever happened.

How could my family not admire these socialist ideals? Most districts had opened free clinics, old-age homes, kindergartens, social welfare offices and centres for adult education. Workers' housing blocks were being built on a grandiose scale and rent controls were at last protecting tenants from rapacious landlords. Not only could workers rent flats at very low rates, but they were also provided with such unheard-of comforts as central heating, gardens, balconies and children's playgrounds. A boy at John's school cut his finger with a penknife to show that he was a red-blooded socialist.

Klara   attended   lectures   on   politics,

psychoanalysis and art, "and dressed with a deliberate lack of elegance, associating especially with those who had suffered the most during the war," according to John. She had a particular fascination for Freud. Both she and Emma did welfare work, inviting poor people in from the street and feeding them, while Richard lectured on Shakespeare's sonnets and English poetry at adult education classes where the fee didn't cover his taxi fare. Among the socialists' anti-clerical gestures was the promotion of cremation as an alternative to the baroque funerals of the past.

John's adored schoolmaster reminisced about the First World War "as the most degrading episode ever known to mankind, hence it could never happen again." This was a widely held sentiment in Vienna where school textbooks "sought to instil love for a country where workers had taken matters in hand, free at last to build their own future." Richard believed that Red Vienna, despite the heavy taxes required to fund its measures for greater social justice, had shown "that even a small beggared nation could march at the forefront of civilisation and reform."

All was not well, however. Business was sluggish, and in fact the only machines busy night and day were the printing presses of the Austro-Hungarian Bank trying to keep up with inflation. The cost-of-living index has risen so high that in 1925 a new Austrian schilling was issued in place of the crown. Anti-semites railed against nefarious "Jewish influences" on the banks and the press. The Social-Democrats' anti-clericalism and contempt for the First World War were not gaining them friends outside Vienna where the country's strongest party, the conservative Christian-Socials, was fast gaining ground.

My grandparents must have been deeply shaken by the riot of July 1927 that followed the unexpected acquittal of two fascists - members of the paramilitary Heimwehr - who had fired into a socialist demonstration outside Vienna, killing a war invalid and a child. In what began as a peaceful demonstration, a furious mob stormed the Palace of Justice and torched it, while police fired at the demonstrators, killing 89 people and wounding hundreds. A first wave of Jewish emigration followed. Wilhelm Reich the controversial psychiatrist witnessed the carnage and saw this as his first encounter with mass hysteria fuelled by what he saw as the release of sexual repression. This, he concluded, was a precursor to the brutalities of the Third Reich.

My Viennese family was noticeably poorer than my family in Czechoslovakia, a fact made obvious to 12-year-old John during a summer reunion in 1928 in the Moravian market town of Vranov to celebrate the Graumann grandparents' 40th wedding anniversary. "Styles clashed," he wrote. "The Brno family was elegant, dad's brother Ferry sometimes dropped by with friends who owned a car, while the Vienna side were still dressed in sackcloth and ashes. It was disturbing to sense Klara and Emma's discomfort."

Father and son: Arthur with baby Bob

Arthur's chic sister Ilka, her husband Edgar and two sons lived in a stylish villa designed by the architect Heinrich Blum. Blum was a close family friend who was to die in a concentration camp, and was among the many Bauhaus-inspired architects whose modernism in the inter-war years reflected the progressive ideas of the newly independent Czechoslovakia. The rich industrial boomtown of Brno is where most of these concrete and glass villas were built, the most famous of those Mies Van der Rohe's exquisite Tugendhat villa.

Bob would play schmaltzy tunes on a toy violin and ask for money

During that same summer holiday, John remembered being much discussed as a "peculiar" child. He memorised thousands of place names around the globe and lists of population statistics, and wrote long letters to his beloved schoolteacher in Vienna. The beautiful Bob, with his blue eyes and brown curls, sang schmaltzy hits while pretending to play his toy violin into which he invited people to drop coins. Of that holiday, what Bob remembered was a delicious sweet on a stick with coconut shavings sprinkled on it.

Bob also remembered a beautifully-bound slim volume that John and all of Vienna's school children received in 1928 to mark the republic's tenth anniversary. "It had a pacifist, humanist message that touched me. I remember one particular story about Austrian soldiers in a dugout on the Russian front around Christmas time. They light a fire to warm themselves by during a lull in the fighting, and as the heat penetrates the earth it wakes the crickets from their winter sleep, and they start chirping, and the soldiers think of home, summer and peace."

Despite Red Vienna's achievements, the aftermath of the 1929 Wall Street crash saw industrial output plummet and unemployment increase. Fascist organisations thrived on people's disaffection, and as no one quite knew where things were headed, the Viennese collected political party membership cards to arm themselves against all eventualities. Having struggled for ten years, the Vienna family sold the disastrously unprofitable Flatter bars and Fritz, Klara and nine-year-old Bus moved to Brno to work for Graumann shoes. The sisters remained close, even after Klara's move, spending most summer holidays together.

My grandparents' situation had greatly improved. Arthur was doing far better than most Viennese and soon better than his relatives on either side of the family because his work was essential to the Vienna operations of Solvay and its local partners. He had a handsome office in the company's Vienna headquarters just off the Ringstrasse, and was head of its small legal department. He also travelled a lot: the complicated post-war legal structures required him to visit government ministries and factories in the former Austro-Hungarian lands, and to go regularly to Belgium, Germany and Italy to assess the international implications of Solvay's work in Vienna.

His boss Eudore Lefèvre was also Belgium's Consul General. Arthur represented the consulate in court, and the two men enjoyed each other's company and had political and philosophical arguments in French. "My father had the grooming and manners to suit the setting," wrote John, "in addition to a personal charm of his own. By a stroke of luck, his pre-war dreams of international law and diplomacy had been vindicated." It would be thanks to Lefèvre that my family left Vienna for Brussels.

Two images of Bob: blue-eyed cupid and lederhausen-wearing Austrian boy

Vienna was still struggling with post-war poverty, and was far from the spruce city it is today. Bob remembered it as dirty and dingy with beggars and crippled war veterans at most street corners and in the parks, and men and women rummaging through the garbage for food. "There was a feeling of hopelessness, people were always talking of the good old days," he wrote in his memoir, which came to me in several instalments through the post the year he felt the urge to put his stories down on paper. "With the exception of the centre around Stephansplatz and Kärntnerstrasse, Vienna was dull and lustreless - grey houses falling to pieces."

There was also a feeling of latent violence, a palpable despair over the post-war situation. He ascribed his life-long dislike of public demonstrations to the dire mood of the time. "I have always hated the mob howling for or against one thing or another. I witnessed too much of it as a child." There were many street demonstrations during Bob's childhood, and many hidden weapons emerged from their caches.

In 1929, when Bob was three, Emma made the decision to leave Vienna's pollution, corruption and frequent unrest, and convinced Arthur to buy a house in the small town of Klosterneuburg beyond the Kahlenberg and Leopoldsberg hills.

The family home in Klosterneuburg long after the war

Klosterneuburg is made up of the German words for "convent" and "new castle", and its chief landmark is a vast monastery in the style of the Escurial outside Madrid, with a Gothic cathedral attached. Today, Klosterneuburg is a placid suburban town with a fine contemporary art museum, where comfortably off Viennese live in villas in the wine-growing hills. But at that time "it was a two-horse town with a sprinkling of Viennese commuters," wrote Bob, "heavily peopled by sympathisers for right-wing causes."

The children now got plenty of fresh air, of which Emma was a keen advocate, but my grandparents' social life depended mostly on visitors from Vienna. Family and friends took the bus or the train, and grandmother Josefine always arrived by taxi. Having agreed somewhat reluctantly to the move, Arthur now stayed in most evenings after work to play the piano. I was told that he read orchestral scores in bed, like books. He was acutely aware of the political developments in Austria, but at the pinnacle of his career as a corporate lawyer he wasn't yet overly concerned about his family's future.

These were the days when Bruno, now a philandering salesman for a large varnish firm in Czechoslovakia, would visit in his chauffeur-driven Tatra and order made-to-measure shirts, and would get the maid to run errands for him. Bruno lived above his means, but Bob greatly approved of him because he would tell the boys to hop into the car and the chauffeur would drive them up the Kahlenberg for ice cream, or for a lavish restaurant meal after a movie. In fact, although all my relatives seem to have been highly critical of one another, no one appears to have disliked generous, larger-than-life Bruno.

Hilde Löwe, second from right, an active member of Vienna's bohemian crowd

The family enjoyed writing light verse. Emma typed poems, or wrote them in tiny handwriting, and they were mostly about family quarrels and reconciliations, but not just. Otto himself had caused great drama and conflicting allegiances by leaving his first wife, the mother of his son, who also happened to be his first cousin. His new love was Hilde Löwe, among Vienna's top piano accompanists and a writer of popular music under the name Henry Love. She was considered very beautiful, and Arthur and Emma invited the new couple over regularly.

Apart from his job, Arthur's main passion was music. Bob remembered that he would return from Vienna, park the car in the garage, walk up the stairs to the living room and sit at the piano. "He usually played Bach, but also many other composers, anything that fell under his hand. He played some passages roughly, but always musically and competently, and entirely for his own enjoyment. Meantime, dinner was cooking in the kitchen and had to be served, but Dad would never interrupt his playing, so a difficult choreography ensued."

"My gracious lady,' the maid used the Austrian formula, "the doctor is reaching the end of his fugue.'

'Quick Hanni,' Emma replied, 'serve now.'

'But I haven't put the parsley butter on the potatoes.'

'Leave it, I'll do it at the table. Oh God, the doctor is starting the next prelude!'

With an expression of controlled despair, Emma plunged the meat back into the oven.

At the table, her exasperation was obvious. Arthur sometimes referred to her as Mater Dolorosa. "She didn't mind when it came from him, but she got very cross if I used the expression," Bob wrote.

Arthur's good fortune appears to have distanced him from former friends, and even if she was proud of his position, Emma wasn't entirely comfortable with it. His family in Czechoslovakia deferred to him, and Emma too always served him the best cuts of meat, and any treat landed on his plate first. But her natural instinct was to side with working-class people, and Arthur's social elevation must have prompted ambivalent feelings.

Except for truces during the holidays, John and Bob hated each other. I can only explain this as jealousy on John's part, who was seven years older. "We were permanently on a war footing," Bob wrote. "John beat me mercilessly about the head, locked me into rooms, kicked my legs, and I did my best to flee or retaliate." He had been so beastly that when they were adults he asked Bob to forgive him.

John was enrolled at Vienna's Schottengymnasium at the age of ten. It was a Catholic school started by Benedictine monks and attended by the upper middle classes, aristocrats, and a sprinkling of converted Jews, among them many years earlier the socialist leader Victor Adler.

The Schottengymnasium's premises behind the Schotten church are where the film director Fritz Lang was baptised and organ concerts are still held. A maze of inner courtyards connects thick-walled buildings where boys clatter down the stairs as though released from prison. There is a café in the first courtyard with an outdoor terrace where Bob and I have drunk coffee and eaten cake, and where Emma bought him an ice cream when he passed the school's entrance exam in 1935.

John's first experience of the school was short-lived. A friend of Emma's spotted him being accidentally knocked down by a taxi as he crossed a Vienna street with a large drawing board under his arm. "I fell, promptly got up and thought nothing of it." But Emma said he was too young to go about on his own in Vienna, and transferred him to the thuggish Klosterneuburg gymnasium, where the painter Egon Schiele had been educated.

There, wearing Lederhosen and a Loden jacket so as not to stand out, John learned to curse profusely. He brought this language home with him, much to his parents' dismay. The teachers spoke crudely and graphically about the war, which made the boys perk up in their seats. He knew, John wrote, that the teachers' roughness was "the consequence of an insane war, compounded by poverty, cynicism, despair and loss of bearings."

In 1931, aged six, Bob was sent to Klosterneuburg's elementary school, "one of the few leftovers of a 19th-century school system", and there was some concern as to how he would mix with the brutish local boys. On his first day, Emma dressed him in a sailor suit with a whistle hanging from a lanyard around his neck, but he wisely left the whistle at home "in case there was a fight". The poverty was such that many of the boys didn't wear leather shoes in the winter, just cardboard, and suffered from impetigo and other skin diseases. The class division between the poor boys and the richer ones was clear; the headmaster beat the poor mercilessly.

The second-grade master was a young man called Richard Zinnecker whom Bob was to loathe for decades after he had left Austria as the embodiment of evil; he too beat the poor and took a sadistic pleasure in his brutality. Bob was among the privileged, as was his friend Burkhard Stifter, whose father ran a small electrical factory and who was to play a key role in Bob's later years. In a class photograph Bob and Burkhard are prominently seated in the middle of the front row, with Burkhard wearing a tie.

Bob recalled a Mothers' Day celebration that angered Emma. The mothers had been invited to the school, where the boys gave them little gifts they had made. "The director then made a speech. 'Have you seen the wrinkles on your mother's hands? Those are from the hard work she is doing for you. One day you will go to a small hill in the cemetery where you poor mother will be buried, and you will cry, but it will be too late, too late to say thank you.'" Some mothers wept into their handkerchiefs, but Emma took Bob home and later told Arthur that the whole thing had lacked taste.

Attitudes were summed up in a ceremony that took place on the occasion of the headmaster's retirement: he and his family sat at a table on a raised stage and ate a full meal featuring fried chicken, while the hungry schoolboys sang folk songs. On witnessing this, Burkhard's father was so incensed that he took some of the poorest boys off to eat hot sausages. Why had socialism made no inroads into Klosterneuburg? Maybe because Austrian socialism appealed to intellectuals and to industrial workers, but the people who lived in small towns were likelier to grieve for the lost empire and look at their German neighbour with envy.

-17-
1930s: When Shakespeare spoke in German

At the ripe old age of 39, my great-uncle Richard passed the entrance exam to the Max Reinhardt theatre school, known as the Seminar. Reinhardt was the most inventive theatrical figure of his day, founder of the Salzburg Festival and among the first directors to be acknowledged as a creative artist. He handled huge casts, divided the stage into an apartment block with rooms on every floor, and made his audiences move around to different stages. His school, subsidised by Austria's Ministry of Education, had rooms in Schönbrunn Palace outside Vienna, using the small baroque Schlosstheater as its stage.

The other students were all in their twenties, but Richard didn't care. "I wanted to see the stage from the wings," he wrote, "to look into its machinery, and to work with actors and experience their difficulties so as to increase my capacity as a translator." He had already translated three or four of Shakespeare's plays, but felt he needed to understand stage production if he was to really master his craft. His two years at the school were the happiest of his life.

Max Reinhardt had a taste for spectacular stage sets

There are many Richards, but the one I want to evoke is the Richard of his heyday, starting to lose his brown hair and self-conscious about the walleye his friends claimed not to notice. His income was small because he didn't work hard as a lawyer, preferring compromise to long drawn-out cases. He had a very comfortable lawyer's office in the Mariahilferstrasse where he spent much time writing, translating or reading his work to friends ensconced on his sofa. Sometimes he spent the night, although he still lived in his mother's house.

With his small nose and lightish colouring, Richard didn't look obviously Jewish. "Gentile friends sometimes told me," he wrote, 'but you aren't a real Jew,' as though they were paying me a compliment." He wondered retrospectively whether he and other "indifferent Jews" – those who didn't look or sound typically Jewish, and didn't practise the Jewish religion - should not always have made a point of stating their origins in the hope of confounding prejudice.

He belonged to the Bach and Vienna Societies, the Weimar Shakespeare Society, as well as a Society for Discharged Convicts that gave released prisoners new clothes and jobs away from Vienna.

Despite being a monarchist, he approved of the changes introduced by Vienna's socialist government, and dismissed Zionism as a reactionary scramble back to the times of Moses and the Maccabees, unless it served as a refuge for persecuted Jews unable to find a home elsewhere.

He was already 36 when he started translating Shakespeare, but he came to believe that this had been his destiny all along and that everything he had done before had led to this moment: the music and theatre, the books he had read. His epiphany came while on holiday in Venice. After a few days spent wandering the canals, he took his copy of *The Merchant of Venice* to bed in the German translation by A W Schlegel, the authority of the day, and was struck by how tortuous and unnatural the language felt.

Back in Vienna, he bought the original play and a few dictionaries and set to work. "It took years," he recalled, "years of mistakes, illusions and self-deception before I found the right way back to Shakespeare, before I learned the translator's task." Shakespeare's diction, he believed, had to be reproduced in German, and he grappled with every comma, exclamation mark and pause to get as close as he could to the original poetry and spontaneity.

Richard translated Shakespeare's plays as well as his sonnets, and in a bilingual edition published in 1934 was the first to juxtapose his work with the originals. His translations were performed at the Burgtheater and the Deutsches Volkstheater in Vienna and the Deutsches Theater in Prague. The 1931 Burgtheater production of his translation of *Measure for Measure* was set in 17th-century Vienna, causing thrilled applause from the first-night audience when the curtains rose on a well-known market square.

Richard the theatre man

So enamoured of Shakespeare was Richard that he also read his translations to audiences by candlelight, first at the homes of friends, later at the Urania, a building by the Danube that by day was a polytechnic but in the evenings lent out its lecture halls. A pianist played interludes for mood changes and to prevent inappropriate bursts of applause. These readings led to invitations to perform at Brno's Masaryk University and at the Workers' Universities where people could attend evening classes in everything from chemistry to languages.

Richard's passion for the English language extended to its poets, and in 1936 he brought out a book in German of poems up to Shelley and Keats, which inspired several composers to set them to music. Two of his translations were printed in Berlin's *Völkischer Beobachter*, the official Nazi newspaper with his name printed on the same page and a bibliography. "I am ashamed when I think that I may be the only Jewish author who ever contributed to that Nazi paper," he wrote.

Richard remained close to Reinhardt after his two years at the Seminar. Reinhardt produced his translation of *A Midsummer Night's Dream* at Schönbrunn's Schlosstheater and later in Salzburg for spectacular open-air performances. He was invited to Reinhardt's rococo palace near Salzburg for candlelit dinners, while flamingos stalked the ponds of its magnificent gardens, and was writing a book for actors and producers about Reinhardt's approach to the theatre.

That was when Germany introduced its Nazi laws ensuring that no publisher could touch a book by a Jew or about a Jew. Richard's translations were banned in Germany, reducing his audience considerably. This didn't slow him down: he wrote four plays, the first about Oliver Cromwell, the second, *Benedeks letzer Sieg* (Benedek's Last Victory) about Ludwig von Benedek, the Austrian general who lost the battle of Königgrätz in the 1866 war against Prussia, and was dismissed, court-martialled and called an idiot by Franz Joseph. Its premiere at Vienna's Deutsches Volkstheater escaped censorship only because the director had silenced would-be hecklers in the stalls by inviting the notorious German ambassador Franz von Papen to the first performance.

His third and most successful play, *Königin Elisabeth,* about the Emperor's wife who had died at the hands of an assassin, ran for many weeks to packed houses. The respected publisher Herbert Reichner was planning to bring out Richard's translations of the complete Shakespeare in instalments over several years. The first beautifully bound volume had been met with critical acclaim shortly before Christmas 1937, and by February 1938 Richard was working on the proofs of the second volume when the Nazis marched into Austria and everything ground to a halt. His adaptation of his own novel about the mind of a murderer was going to be performed at the Burgtheater, and that was cancelled.

"When I left Austria, I lost my homeland. Vienna had given me music, a sense of beauty, the idea of justice. I loved the mountains of Austria and the lakes and meadows for I had been happy there, happier than I can say in words. But deeply as it hurts to be homeless, there is one thing that cuts deeper still; that I lost my work, the one work which had made my life worth living." After he arrived in London, he fell into a deep gloom.

It was in London, while recovering from recurrent bouts of fever at St Albans hospital, that a doctor asked Richard why he hadn't had his eye fixed; the operation was easy and painless. Richard pondered the idea overnight but the next day told the doctor he would rather not. The defect was a part of him and, like being a Jew, it had given him a more interesting outlook on life - a minority's perspective.

Non-violent anti-Jewish prejudice "has always been a wholesome stimulus just as my squint has been to me," Richard argued. Anti-semitism was what had unified a diverse population that would otherwise have assimilated. "A minority that in the short period since its admittance to equal rights – hardly more than a hundred years – has produced such famous men as Mendelssohn, Disraeli, Einstein and Freud has no need to apologise for its existence."

"After all," he wrote, "God wanted me to be a Jew, He evidently wished me to carry that burden, not to throw it away, or to ease its weight cunningly."

Because he didn't have children, recollections of Richard are those of his nephews. Bob remembered him from his Vienna boyhood as a soft-voiced man who took an interest in him, but they rarely saw each other after the Second World War. By then Richard had returned to Vienna, where he married the sister of a childhood friend. When my uncle John and Bus mention Richard in their memoirs they are resentful, if not angry, that he kept telling them what to do. He wasn't their father.

But I can see from Richard's memoirs the man who wept at the theatre, the intellectual who conducted epistolary conversations about Hamlet with Sigmund Freud and about Shakespeare in general with the satirist Karl Kraus. He also wrote anti-Nazi political columns for the *Wiener Zeitung*, the Austrian government's newspaper, as well as many "feuilletons": personal essays Austrian newspapers carry on the lower half of the front page, and which Karl Kraus fustigated as the lowest form of journalism.

More crucial to his survival, as it turned out, he doubled as the newspaper's legal adviser in several lawsuits against Nazis, and the paper's editor Dr Pankraz Kruckenhauser was a friend. After the Anschluss, Kruckenhauser turned out to have been an active underground Nazi. Richard was astonished; he had no idea that this Tyrolean intellectual was anything but pro-Austrian. They had spent long hours in cafés discussing books and ideas.

"Now I understood why he had made such extensive use of me," Richard wrote, "why he had published almost all my political articles with my full name, and why he had made me the paper's legal representative. He did not want to expose an Aryan lawyer to those perils: a Jew was just the right man for that job."

Richard wondered why after the Anschluss the Gestapo hadn't come looking for him at once, when other journalists were not so lucky. Another Jewish journalist on the *Wiener Zeitung* swallowed poison together with his mother, while a friend threw himself out a window. Later, he thought, perhaps Kruckenhauser had remembered a private legal bill Richard had never sent and had given him enough time to get out of Vienna.

I am not exactly sure when or why Richard ended up in Vienna in his later years. In his memoirs he wrote that he would never return to his homeland because he wouldn't know what the person who was shaking his hand had done a few years earlier. Something happened to change his mind, maybe the offer of a stipend from the state, and belated recognition of his work. It must have been painful to go back to this city of death, and strange too to be in Vienna at the same time as his brother-in-law Arthur who had also returned, and not see each other. Richard achieved recognition, though, and Arthur did not.

The 25 translations of Shakespeare published after the war in six volumes by the German publisher Kurt Desch were followed in the late 1950s by 154 sonnets. When Richard died in 1960, aged 69, he had seen his greatest wish fulfilled. "What I have wished and hoped for is one thing only: that I might live to see my Shakespeare translations rounded off and published. Then I should not care tuppence whether in Austria or Germany there is anti-semitism or not; whether they take notice of my work or not. I should have done what I thought my duty, that's all."

-18-

1930s: As dark clouds gather

What came to be known as Austro-Fascism echoed the most conservative elements within the Catholic clergy. In March 1933, after a row over voting procedures, Chancellor Engelbert Dollfuss dismissed the Austrian Parliament. This freed him from a number of headaches, including a possible alliance with the socialists he loathed, even though they might have helped him confront the Nazi menace. From then on he ruled by decree.

Bob, although only a boy, thought himself extremely fond of Dollfuss, who because of his size was nicknamed Millimetternich. He knew the pious peasant was not popular among the adults of his family, "but he was about my size when I was ten, and for that reason and because of the powerful propaganda we were exposed to at school, I liked the man."

Dollfuss visited Klosterneuburg for one the many speeches he gave that year. Hitler was now chancellor of Germany, and Dollfuss was doing all he could to defend Austria's independence from the Reich. The school children were assembled in the square that then carried his name. They had been ordered to wear an insignia with the Austrian colours and the Chancellor's words, *Seid einig* (be united). "But this cost one groschen, and many could not afford it, so only the wearers were placed in front. The speech was endlessly dull, with much mention of the Vaterland, loyalty and the duties of the future generation."

"I knew that my mother and Otto sympathised with the socialists," Bob wrote. "This bothered me because socialists had a bad reputation at my school." The Austro-nationalist brainwashing of schoolboys was intensive but not subtle. "We were told much about the world war and the courage and suffering of the soldiers; the socialists were described as godless and immoral; the church was in vogue. They didn't seem to have any model in their minds of a small, partly German-speaking country that respected itself, although Switzerland would have been a good example."

Emma thought Bob gave himself airs. One day she caught him using the expensive transparent English soap in Richard's bathroom, and scolded him for his luxurious tastes. She herself was a far earthier person, who enjoyed getting into abusive verbal sparring matches with the market people in the colourful Viennese dialect.

"We paid little attention to the ridiculous guttersnipe and his seemingly unimportant access to the government of Germany," her eldest boy John wrote of Hitler. At that stage my grandparents would still have been convinced that Hitler was not going to last. This was also, John believed, a good period in his parents' marriage, when they went by car on a long summer holiday to Zurich and Paris, and then again to Yugoslavia.

Austria had what were virtually two private armies, the Heimwehr (home defence), close to the Christian-Socials, and the Social-Democrats'

Schutzbund. These were frequently engaged in country-wide skirmishes. After dismissing Parliament, Dollfuss banned the Schutzbund, forcing it underground. Backed by the clergy and the now legalised Heimwehr, he replaced the democratic constitution with a corporate Catholic one modelled on Mussolini's. Mussolini, who had once been a street sweeper in Vienna, was Austria's ally at this point, wanting Austria to act as a buffer between Italy and Nazi Germany.

In September, Dollfuss set up the Fatherland Front (Vaterländische Front), which merged his Christian-Socials with the Heimwehr, and outlawed the communist and Nazi parties. In the meantime, Germany was arming and bankrolling Austria's underground Nazis. Working in small SS and SA cells, they dynamited bridges, roads and telegraph

Bob near the time of the Anschluss

installations, and murdered. By defending Austria's independence, Dollfuss had alienated the pro-German Austrians.

Nazi acts of violence were a daily occurrence, but despite the ugly political atmosphere John was emerging at last from his gloom. When his relationship with Emma reached a crisis point, he was sent for several months to a boarding house on the Semmering mountain range south of Vienna, and returned transformed into an energetic, even hyperactive adolescent. He was eating ravenously, hiking and cycling, running up the Leopoldberg hill and down again, relishing the cold and the physical effort, and looking forward to university. He was discovering how much he loved Austria, its hills and woods, and holidays on the lakes in the Austrian Alps.

Austria had vast numbers of hidden weapons, unreturned after the end of the First World War or the result of the illegal arms trade with Italy, and these were either in the hands of the Heimwehr or of the Schutzbund. Bob's cousin Peter remembered his mother's minor involvement. "A socialist friend gave my mother a revolver, which she hid in my toy drawer. A few weeks later he gave her another gun. It was the real thing this time; the first had been a toy to test her dependability."

Vienna's socialist years were to end in bloodshed in February 1934, when a raid on a workers' club in the city of Linz spread like wildfire into a three-day civil war. The fighting in Vienna was the fiercest. On February 12, the socialists called for a general strike and martial law was declared. The Schutzbund was known to have hidden weapons in the estates of Vienna's working-class suburbs. Using this as a pretext, Dollfuss shelled the buildings with artillery fire, despite the women and children inside.

Bob, who was eight, remembered from his home in Klosterneuburg hearing canon firing at the Karl-Marx-Hof, and was frightened. The model workers' estates were viewed by some as threatening fortresses of plebeian revolution. Not everyone was aware of the tragedy unfolding. Stefan Zweig who lived in the city centre was unaware of the drama until he read the evening papers.

Hundreds of people died, among them many women and children; others hid for safety in Vienna's sewers or fled, and many more were made homeless and destitute. Eleven men were tried and hanged shortly afterwards, and scores of people were sent to concentration camps on charges of high treason.

For the British journalist G. E. R. Gedye reporting from Vienna for *The Times* of London, "What I could not forget throughout that night of horror was that I was forced to be present at the ruthless destruction (...) of a great and world-recognised example of what could be done by devoted idealists and scientific reformers to give the masses of my fellow-beings something of the good things in life which I demanded for myself - clean homes, sunshine, pure air, a glimpse of green from at least some of their windows, decent sanitation, a corner of safety from traffic for the children to play in."

Otto was deeply affected by this hounding of Austria's socialists. A flurry of decrees had systematically chipped away at social protection, and while wage earners were losing many of their rights, landlords had been allowed to increase rents. Dollfuss invested money in his peasant followers in the provinces at the expense of Vienna's working classes, and cultural and sports organisations were closed one after another.

In his memoirs, Richard quotes from articles he wrote for the *Wiener Zeitung* after the Night of the Long Knives, June 30-July 2, 1934, when Hitler ordered some 85 political executions of the Sturmabteilug (SA), the paramilitary Brownshirts, and other critics of his regime. Among them was his one-time close ally and co-founder of the SA, Ernst Röhm, who died riddled with bullets in his prison cell. Richard wrote an emotional column after Hitler's July 1934 speech to the Reichstag.

"It is said that on Friday night Hitler's voice trembled with agitation. Rightly it may have done so. Röhm's seat on the ministers' bench was empty.

Among the MPs almost a dozen seats were frighteningly empty. They were empty because of the 'Führer's wish'. It is said that several times during his speech Hitler hit the desk with his clenched fist. The whole of civilised mankind heard that fist. It hits hard. Its bang reverberates throughout the world. One single voice could have drowned the rant from that mouth and the rumble of that fist. It could drown that hubbub at any time, if only it would speak. But we do not hear that voice - the voice of Germany's conscience."

-19-

1934: The mood changes

The mood in Vienna changed significantly after the Night of the Long Knives. A coal-starved Italy had switched sides and was now allied with Germany, and Hitler had the military's endorsement, which increased his power. And yet after the millions of people killed in the First World War, most of my family still believed that the western powers would intervene to make Germany return to a civilised form of government.

John remembered his mother Emma taking him aside and saying, "this might even concern us." He misunderstood, replying that "this concerned everybody. This concerns the whole world, who on earth wants to have a bloody war again? If those Prussians are not stopped right away, there will be hell and bloodshed as never before."

"No, she said, not only that. There is another thing, namely that we are Jews, hastening to add that we were assimilants. I nodded emphatically, for I was perennially in leather pants and mastered the Viennese dialect to perfection. She added that this was all right because there were many honourable, even distinguished Jews, and rarely any depraved deviants such as drunkards, rapists, thieves or murderers."

"The subject never came up again between my parents and me. I know that for my father Jews were in the third person, whether good or bad, just as any other kind of people. We were Czechoslovakians, German-speaking, the less fortunate descendants of a cultured greater Austria, marginal Christians, and free to invent a philosophy of our own."

The socialist leader Otto Bauer had found refuge in Brno in Czechoslovakia, smuggled out of Austria in army uniform, from where he kept the party alive. Dollfuss failed to come to an arrangement with the Nazis, as he had hoped, and on July 25, 1934, ten Nazis burst into his office at the Chancellory, shot him twice and let him bleed slowly to death. The plotters were arrested and tried, and the quiet, devout lawyer Kurt von Schuschnigg took over, as intent as Dollfuss had been on safeguarding Austria's independence. The two leaders of the putsch were hanged in a verdict that infuriated Germany's Nazis.

Lomnice was a favourite place for the family to holiday, with Emma, Bob and Ilka in dark dress

That summer my family gathered together in its ancestral Czech village of Lomnice for Otto and Hilde's last summer before they were to leave for England. "The news from Vienna," wrote John, "was that a bunch of degenerate Nazis had murdered the black fascist chancellor Dollfuss, but that he had been promptly replaced by Schuschnigg, a good man, and so much the better."

My family saw Dollfuss as the tyrant who had ruthlessly crushed the socialists, a fascist who had deserved to die at the hands of fellow fascists. Schuschnigg hadn't been involved in the civil uprising's bloodbath, and they believed he could restore democracy.

That his family rejoiced at Dollfuss's murder made Bob feel deeply conflicted. "I was distressed because I loved Dollfuss, and I was horrified that the murderers had let him bleed to death, even refusing him the assistance of a priest." Like Dollfuss, Schuschnigg's driving ambition was to keep the Nazis at bay and maintain Austria's independence. He hated the socialists as much as Dollfuss had, even though at one point they represented 42 percent of Vienna's voters.

The crushing of the socialists distressed Otto more deeply than the then prevailing anti-semitism. His girlfriend Hilde had during her concerts tours come to know an eccentric Irish society lady, Molly Miller-Mundy, who was to make their escape from Austria possible. Miller-Mundy, a wealthy flame-haired amateur singer, hired Hilde to be her private piano accompanist in London, where she lived. Hilde moved first and Otto followed, having packed up many of his paintings along with the toy puppet theatre.

Otto arose early on his first day in London because he wanted to see the paintings at the National Gallery, but was greeted by thick smog outside the front door. When he reached the museum, the smoke-polluted fog made it "look like a nobleman's country house whose foundations had subsided. In the gallery I searched for works of the British school, but my eyes began to burn as I stood before Gainsborough's *Miss Siddons*. The painting receded, and finally disappeared behind a thick yellow veil."

He could barely see. A museum guard warned Otto that this was a pea-soup fog and that he had better leave before it got worse. "Like a blind man I groped my way along, keeping close to the walls. I could see legs step out before me but not the bodies belonging to them." He eventually made it back to his lodgings, and sat by the flickering light of an ineffective coal fire. The tar-smelling air was as dark and depressing as the political mood.

But despite the pollution, London was a blast of fresh air after Vienna. "I saw no poverty, but well dressed, happy people," Otto wrote. "Some were queuing at bus stops in self-imposed discipline. Passers-by apologised when they inadvertently touched you. Young men and women in evening dress walked amidst the crowd, and no one seemed to envy them or begrudge them their gaiety. How different all this was to the behaviour of people at home."

"My father had contempt for the increasing corruption of the Austrian state," wrote John. "He could afford to because he was Czech and because he worked for an international company." Arthur's Steyr 200 was not only a status symbol, but also his means of escape. His hometown of Brno was a two-hour drive from Vienna along the pot-holed Austrian roads and the smooth Czech ones, and he liked to visit on Sundays, often taking the boys along. Emma stayed in Vienna because she didn't get on with her mother-in-law.

After his unfortunate spell at Klosterneuburg's primitive grammar school, John was back at the elite Schottengymnasium, "a return to civilisation." In 1935, aged nine, Bob too became a dayboy there. Most of the teachers were priests, and the school was a centre of moderate conservatism, with strong loyalties to the Habsburg family. My grandparents had registered their sons' religion as Catholic at birth and this even before they themselves had converted. Whether the school knew their origins I don't know, but I suppose they did.

On one of his later visits to Vienna Bob became curious about his school record and went to the Schottengymnasium's secretariat to ask if they still had his reports from the 1930s, and those of his brother. "*Bist du jüdisch?*" the woman in charge had eagerly asked, with a sympathetic smile, realising that he had left in 1938. Bob was struck by her amicable interest, and noted with interest when he read the reports that John's results were not as outstanding as he had expected.

It was Arthur's brother-in-law Edgar, the Czech insurance agent with the spooky hand, who first made John aware that his father Arthur was a reluctant Jew. He nicknamed the blue-eyed, light-haired John a "show Goy", like the handful of Aryan boys among the Jewish boy scouts who stopped them from appearing to be segregated. "There's a piece of pork in this family," he said on another occasion, looking at Arthur and laughing uproariously.

My grandfather was probably not amused. A dapper, outwardly confident man of 43, Arthur had been feeling increasingly comfortable in the well-polished shoes of a Viennese liberal intellectual. When not travelling he enjoyed a daily routine; a shave at the barber's, and breakfast in the dark-panelled rooms of Café Landtmann where the waiters greeted him with a respectful "Herr

Graumann" and where he would read the newspapers on their wooden holders, before a short stroll to the Solvay offices off the Schottenring, past the liveried doorman and through its hallowed halls to his own office.

Until the Anschluss, Bob had been unaware of his Jewish origins. He had seen himself as a little Lord Fauntleroy, a book he'd read as *Der Kleine Lord*. I'm not sure how well that image tallies with the lederhosen-wearing son of a socialist mother, but that's what he told me. "I didn't know what it meant to be a Jew. I thought Jews belonged to a minority religion, and that perhaps some family members were Jewish. Now I found I belonged to a dangerous, hated race."

In view of the insecure political situation, Arthur decided that, having obtained his school-leaving certificate, the *Matura*, John should study economics in Prague instead of Vienna. For that he would need the Czech Matura. Outside work, Arthur was spending less and less time in Vienna, playing the piano in Klosterneuburg and reading books about religious philosophy. In the meantime, John enrolled briefly at Vienna's University of Economics.

"But the merciless persecution of socialists after 1934, and the gradual emigration of Jewish faculty had deprived the school of any teaching staff worth mentioning." John relaxed, as he knew he would be heading for Prague's school of economics in the next term. "Czechoslovakia was more dignified, and I was proud that my four grandparents had come from there. Honest, unpretentious, with its magnificent pine forests, it spoke with a deeper voice and more profound sense."

Otto made a lightning visit to Vienna from London in 1936 to deal with remaining business and to collect some belongings, and came face to face with everything he loathed and feared. His studio was on the fourth floor of a block of flats in Döbling, across the landing from a middle-aged couple, Herr and Frau M, whose portraits he had painted.

"After the removal van had taken away the last piece of furniture, I went to our neighbour's door and rang the bell," he wrote. "Frau M received me with unexpectedly cool formality." She asked him into the drawing room, then abruptly rushed to the adjoining room and slammed the door. "She was too late; through the gap of the half-open door I had glimpsed the portrait of Adolf Hitler." National Socialism was still illegal at the time, and Frau M may have feared that Otto would denounce her husband to the police.

"Frau M's face had reddened, her hands trembled and she had to sit down. It was perhaps petty of me to take revenge on the little woman sitting before me. Oratory was never my strong side. On this occasion, however, I talked as if Europe was listening at my feet. Hitler means war, I said, and Hitler's war means world war; Germany's towns will crumble into dust, millions will die, your Führer will drag you down, will burden you with unforgivable guilt, and if you do not die you will curse the man you so much admire until the bitter end of your life. My last words were 'Tell your husband he is a damned fool.'"

-20-

1938: Anschluss

The Nazis' infiltration of Austria intensified, and swastikas appeared on walls even though the government had banned them. Nazi thugs in black motorcycle jackets went roaring up and down the streets. Twelve-year-old Bob listened to the radio obsessively. "You heard Hitler's speeches, so violent, so aggressive, so stupid," he said. "Jews were in a conspiracy against Germany. Germany was waging a war on the Jews."

In early 1938, Arthur was planning to move to the new Solvay offices in Prague. On February 12, Hitler summoned Chancellor Schuschnigg to Berchtesgaden, his Eagles' Nest, where he received him with rudeness and contempt. After having made him wait, forbidden him from smoking and yelling at him, he ordered the Austrian chancellor to amnesty all jailed Austrian Nazis and to bring two Nazis into his government.

On his return, a shaken but partly resigned Schuschnigg placed two prominent Nazis in government and released the jailed Nazis, but restated his vow to preserve Austria's independence. He gave a stirring speech to Parliament.

A furious Hitler ordered the illegal Austrian Nazis to foment further disorder throughout the country. At very short notice, so as to prevent the Third Reich from sabotaging its results, Schuschnigg ordered a plebiscite that asked Austrian citizens the simple question, "Are you in favour of the independence of Austria or not?"

Richard was at the Burgtheater when this was announced. "I read the proclamation beneath a lamppost, and I remember being torn between joy and fear, hope and foreboding. The Austrians entertained no illusions as to the Nazis' true character - the cutting of telephone wires, the daily bombs - but they wanted to put an end to the stress of never-ending disorder."

Hitler sent angry ultimatums ordering that the plebiscite be called off, and when Schuschnigg refused to do so he sent troops to Austria's border. On March 11, Schuschnigg resigned as chancellor in a radio broadcast that was to be remembered by all Austrians who heard it, ending with the sentence, "So I take my leave of the Austrian people, with the German word of farewell, uttered from the depth of my heart - God protect Austria." There followed the melancholy strains of Austria's national anthem, followed by Schubert's Unfinished Symphony. The battle for independence had been lost.

A friend rang Richard with the news that Schuschnigg had resigned and that Hitler was marching in. He had been putting the finishing touches to his translation of *The Tempest*. Questions raced through his mind. "I paced up and down. Should I go abroad at once? What about my mother? Should I burn my anti-Hitler writings? The room was dark save for the lamp on my writing table. It was a big room with three windows. There stood my bookcase, and a huge cupboard from

Maria Theresa's day. Over there was the glass case with my collection of china, cut glass and miniatures. On the other side the round table with the old settee where I used to read my translations to my friends. The portraits of my parents looked down at me from the walls, and I gazed up at my father, so many years dead, yet still alive in my heart. What would he say? Would he advise me to bid farewell to Austria? Here, this room was my Austria, here I had worked and been happy."

"That Friday afternoon (March 11) I was alone in the house with my father," wrote John. "Mother and Bob were at a concert in the city, and the maids were out. Father turned on the radio for the news. Without a word we listened to the end, then father turned the radio off. 'Poor Austria', he said, and I knew he meant the former, bigger Austria, not the pitiful republic of my times. Then he paced up and down until Emma and Bob came home, fretting that they were out on the roads."

Bob remembered that fateful evening slightly differently. "I had been doing my homework upstairs and vaguely knew this was a day when Arthur came home early so that Emma could take the car and go to the opera with her friend Frau Danzer. I came downstairs and found Dad drinking tea and listening to the radio. I heard the concluding words, God protect Austria. This was not unusual language in those days, but Dad said, "This is it. It's all over." Later he found Arthur pacing nervously and saying that Emma had not chosen the ideal evening to go to Vienna.

It didn't take long for the streets of Vienna to be filled with screaming hate-filled crowds. The British journalist Gedye reported that when racing to his office he was met by "an indescribable witches' sabbath - stormtroopers, lots of them barely out of the schoolroom, marching side by side with police turncoats, men and women shrieking or crying the name of their leader (...) leaping, shouting and dancing in the light of the smoking torches: 'Down with the Jews! Heil Hitler! Sieg Heil! Perish the Jews! Hang Schuschnigg!"

The shouting and madness erupted in Klosterneuburg too. "As soon as night fell, we heard howling and yelling in the streets," Bob wrote. "An endless procession of torch bearers shuffled past, shouting *"Ein Volk, ein Reich, ein Führer*! Emma returned after I had gone to bed. During the intermission she had heard rumours that things were happening, and had made it home without mishap."

The next day, Emma took John to buy swastika flags for the janitor who lived in their home to display in her windows as everyone except Jews and foreigners had to do so, and they were surprised to see the shops already full of them. Within two days, the streets were awash with flags, and there were flowers at every lamppost. In the streets, people greeted each other with the Nazi salute and wore the Greater Germany badge in their buttonholes, a swastika next to an enlarged map of Germany. Young people in white knee socks sang martial Nazi songs, while at the same time desperate men and women from all walks of life were trying to flee Austria by plane, train, car, and even on foot through the mountain passes.

Schuschnigg was succeeded as Chancellor by the Nazi party's Arthur Seyss-Inquart, one of the two Nazis he had brought into his government, and who was to be hanged at Nuremberg for the crimes he later committed in Holland. When the German troops arrived on March 12 they were greeted by cheering, swastika-waving crowds, their arms feverishly raised in salute. The next day, the Anschluss incorporated Austria into the German Reich.

Hitler was to declare his annexation to fervent throngs from the balcony of the Habsburg Palace in the Heldenplatz. Overhead photographs of that March 15 address show a tight mass of pinheads gathered in the square, almost half a million supporters. The police stood tolerantly by. As Vienna's Jews listened on their radios to the hectoring voice and the rapturous roars, they realised they were going to be scapegoated for the frustrations and pent-up anger built up during Austria's years of economic hardship.

Richard recalls making the laborious way to his office on the day of Hitler's arrival. The street was lined on each side with three rows of policemen, soldiers and Storm Troopers, the latter facing the house windows to make sure they were closed, while church bells rang in wild abandon. Hitler arrived several hours' behind schedule, steadying himself with his left hand on the window screen as he stood in his car, his head moving mechanically from right to left and back again, his right arm stretched in the Nazi salute. Had it not been for a waft of death, wrote Richard, he would merely have seemed ridiculous, but "he looked like a mechanical image of himself, the full-size image of a dreadful deity of destruction."

How did one reconcile the assumption that most Austrians wanted independence from Germany with the wild reception the Germans received? Richard asked. After the Anschluss, he wrote, "they'd felt greatly relieved that they had not missed the bus and became - all of a sudden - good Nazis." Because most Viennese had hedged their bets by collecting party membership cards, they adapted to the new situation quite smoothly.

Bob's cousin Peter remembered the shock and disbelief among family members and Jewish friends. They had felt so fully assimilated, far away from the world of shtetls, pogroms and terror, often even denying their origins. "They saw themselves first and foremost as German-Austrians," Peter wrote. "Had they not contributed massively to the culture, sciences and economic development of the country and had they not fought as patriots in the First World War? They wanted to believe that the explosion of violent anti-semitism would soon burn itself out."

Arthur's Belgian boss was reassigned to the company's Brussels headquarters and suggested that Arthur join him there. With the fear of war, Solvay was preparing for the post-war salvage of its central European factories. Under Nazi rules, Jewish staff in Germany and Austria was forced to resign. Solvay's in-house historian in Brussels says the company tried to find other jobs for most of them.

Like many Jewish boys, Bob and John didn't yet fully understand that these men were the enemy, but instead saw them as an embodiment of the martial ideals they had grown up admiring. Bob was fascinated by the German troops with their resplendent cars and motorcycles. Even the older John shared this patriotic pride at the sight of these handsome young men and their shining machines. The Germans took over the large military barracks in Klosterneuburg, a leftover from the days of empire. Squadrons of warplanes flew overhead, their deafening drone creating a stultifying effect.

The Graumanns' musician neighbours and friends the Walters received visits from German officers because the organist Karl Walter was a

Rhinelander. Bob wrote that these officers were all anti-Nazi. Emma succumbed to a brief nervous breakdown, lying in bed for several days of despondency. "At a time when we in Austria knew no more about the future than any ignorant western political leaders," wrote Bob, "she must have sensed intuitively that something terrible lay ahead."

But she came back to life and actively started helping friends and family find ways of getting out of Vienna. Within a few weeks of the Anschluss, Peter's mother Eva was making daily visits to the British Embassy's consular section. Only later did Peter realise she had been expecting his visa for England, his father Otto having signed the necessary documents. "It did not occur to me then that my father had refused to do the same for my mother, and that she had decided to make the sacrifice of parting with me to ensure my safety."

It didn't take Austria's Nazis very long - in fact the day the Anschluss was declared - to display their hatred of the Jews with far more savagery than the Germans. Old men were forced to scrub pavements, acid was thrown into the water buckets; Jews were made to sweep the streets before jeering crowds, sidelocks were snipped amid laughter, shopkeepers made to sit in their shop windows wearing insulting notices around their necks. The public displays of anti-semitism were so unrestrained and sadistic that the only hope was to get out as fast as one could, if one could. Klara returned to Prague from a visit to Vienna having witnessed blood-chilling acts.

Bob was protected by his Czech nationality, but his cousin Peter, being Austrian, had had to move to a school for Jewish children. "It was in the Schottengasse and we were given some haphazard lessons," he wrote. "When the summer vacation came I was sent to the countryside with my two girl cousins." In early June, the mansion where he had lived until then with his mother and her family was requisitioned as an SS headquarters.

A few days later, 18-year-old John was boarding a train for Brno to stay with his aunt Ilka, where he was to prepare for his Czech exams. He was still certain the Nazis would be brought to heel by France and the Soviet Union. "There was concern of course," he wrote, "with the indignities to which the Nazis had begun to expose the Jews of Vienna, revolting by any standards of decency."

He discussed these events with his uncle Bruno, who also lived in Brno, and "naively I sought to assure him that except under the Nazis one has no need to be a Jew, since all depends on how one thinks about this. I for one was not a Jew, whatever the Nazis might say. '*Grosser Gott!*' my aunt Bruno's wife said, 'what do you think you are if not a Jew?' But soon I saw my cousin Bus and he explained to me that under Nazi laws one is defined as a Jew unless one can prove that not one of one's grandparents had been a Jew."

John's ambivalent statement shows how far removed he felt from his ancestry. Like other Jews who emigrated to the United States, and like the family of his future wife, he did not want to be identified as Jewish. One of my cousins says he grew up feeling that his dark eyes and strong nose were an embarrassment to his parents, compared to his brother and sister's blue eyes. John was a brilliant but troubled man, and his experience of exile did little to reinforce his sense of possessing a rightful place in the world.

Wearing a little Czechoslovak flag on his lapel, rather than a Jewish star, Bob went on attending the Schottengymnasium. The Czech flag meant that he could walk in the streets without being attacked. "In each classroom, there was a picture of Hitler next to the cross, and every lesson started after the teacher had raised an arm in the Nazi salute and said Heil Hitler! The children had to reply the same way - with the exception of foreigners and Jews. All the monks and most of the lay teachers looked unhappy, although one or two had bright, shiny faces."

In May, Austria introduced the Nuremberg racial laws, and anti-semitic regulations deprived Jews of their basic human rights. Jewish doctors, lawyers, scientists, politicians, civil servants, teachers, actors and musicians could no longer work. Works by Jewish artists, composers and writers could not be performed or sold. Jewish shops were closed or "Aryanised". As persecuted, destitute Jews arrived in Vienna from the provinces, the Jewish community was allowed to work again to help organise their mass migration. By the summer, Jews were required to take the first name "Sara" or "Israel", and were banned from public parks, public transport, cinemas and on and on.

"I quickly learned that being Jewish was not limited to those professing that religion," Bob wrote. "I learned about the daily battles for visas to get out, and the nightmarish red tape that had to be fought to be allowed to leave. I heard about the transports to Dachau and the desperate struggle of women to obtain a visa to anywhere in the world because that was the only way to get their husbands out of the concentration camp. I also heard about the first deaths in the camps, and the ashes that were sent to the families, who were asked to pay for them."

Richard received a circular from the Vienna

Goethe Society calling members to say whether they were "Aryan" or "non-Aryan"; the society's founder, a Jewish university professor, had died just before the Anschluss. A circular from the Society for Discharged Convicts asked their Jewish members to resign. Richard wrote a postcard back saying he refused to resign, but that they were welcome to strike him off their list if they didn't want his contributions anymore. A third note from the Minister of Justice was much more serious, informing him that he would no longer be allowed to work as a lawyer. "There was nothing for me, had I stayed on, other than starving to death or suicide."

The first priority now for Emma was to find a buyer for the Klosterneuburg house. Arthur had gone ahead to Brussels, and Emma was also making plans for her mother in Brigittenau; gentile neighbours promised they would check on her regularly. The Klosterneuburg villa went for very little money as many Austrians saw the persecution of Jews as an ideal opportunity for bargains. They were lucky to have been able to leave early enough to sell anything at all. The Austrians were quick to expropriate and pillage Jewish property, or "Aryanise" it, from department stores like Rosenberger's to the Prater's Ferris wheel and cafes owned by Jews.

-21-

Flight

In August 1938, SS Lieutenant Adolf Eichmann set up Vienna's Central Office for Jewish Emigration. Its aim was to strip Jews of their money, homes and possessions in exchange for a passport ordering them to leave Austria. But no one could leave without a visa, while without a guarantor in the country of destination there would be no visa. Endless queues formed outside foreign consulates, hundreds, sometimes thousands of desperate people hoping for a means of escape.

Amidst the horror one man's stand is worth singling out. He was Feng-Shan Ho, the youthful Chinese Consul General, whose name is among those of the Righteous people recognised by Israel's Holocaust memorial centre Yad Vashem. An orphan from Huan Province, Ho held a PhD in political economy from the University of Munich. He served in Vienna from 1938 to 1940, issuing visas to Shanghai. In fact, Shanghai did not require visas, but they served the purpose of satisfying Nazi demands for proof of emigration.

Ho continued despite orders to stop from the Kuomintang's Ambassador to Berlin who wanted to strengthen his country's ties with Germany. When the consulate building was confiscated by the Nazis because it was Jewish-owned, he moved to another office paying for the costs out of his own pocket and continuing to sign visas until he was ordered back to the Republic of China in May 1940. He is believed to have saved the lives of 12,000 Viennese Jews.

Bob's cousin Peter was never to know where his mother, grandmother and great-grandmother went after the SS requisitioned their huge family home in Vienna. His visa arrived as soon as he had returned from the countryside, and hasty arrangements were made for his departure. His grandmother had found money for his air ticket. "I clearly remember the scene on the spectator's terrace at Vienna's Aspern airfield where my mother, grandmother and I were waiting for the flight to be called, but it did not occur to me that I might be parting with them for good."

He was about to board the Junker Ju 52 Lufthansa plane with 20 or so other passengers when a uniformed man grabbed him and marched him to an office. The money his mother had tried to slip into his pocket was confiscated, but they let him go. "What must my mother and grandmother have felt when they saw me taken back to the terminal? And the relief to see me hurry back and get on the waiting plane!" The flight to Croyden Airport took seven hours with four stopovers, and he was sick all the way. Otto picked him up and asked sharply, as if it was Peter's fault, "Did you know there were swastikas on the wings of your plane?"

Meanwhile, my grandfather Arthur had told John to come straight back to Vienna. There was not going to be any studying in Prague; he was to join the family in Brussels. But first he must say goodbye to his Czech relatives. In Brno, Arthur's brother and sister said they were disappointed that Arthur would not be moving there for his job; they had been looking forward to it. They themselves had no plans for leaving Czechoslovakia. They did not want to live among strangers.

In Prague, Arthur's other brother Fritz and Emma's sister Klara were intent on getting their son Bus out of Czechoslovakia, but had no plans to leave the country themselves. John found them tuned in to the radio in their apartment, listening to stations across Europe and particularly to Moscow, where the news gave them little hope.

"A way had to be found to get my cousin Bus to go west," wrote John, "but as for Fritz and Klara, they had long agreed they did not wish to be a burden on the family." My other explanation for the Czech family's passivity is that they they felt relatively safe as Czechs because they had faith in president Edvard Benes, a university professor who had co-founded the Republic with Tomas Masaryk, and headed its democratic government for 20 years. They were relieved not to live in Vienna.

With the Klosterneuburg house sold, Emma and 11-year-old Bob boarded a train for Brno, then Prague, and from there a Sabena plane to Brussels. That was the last time they would see their Czech relatives. "From this moment on my parents lived the life of exiles in four countries," wrote Bob, "in none of which they took root. Although both returned to Austria after the war, only Dad died there. Emigration, like revolution, does not benefit the first generation."

In Vienna, playwright Richard spent the months after the Anschluss trying to leave legally, as he believed this would spare his mother problems. He recalled an exchange with a young Nazi official at the income tax office, where he had to settle his tax bill. When he had filled in the papers, the official asked him, if the question was not too indiscreet, where he was going to live. "I'll go to England," Richard said.

"Of course, as a Shakespeare translator you'll make a lot of money over there."

"I suppose so."

"So this emigration doesn't mean very much, does it?"

Richard felt his blood boil. He leaned over the table.

"Do you really think so? Do you really think it does not matter to me where I live? Does not matter that I have to leave my mother behind? The town where I was born? My work? My friends? Isn't there something that is called a man's home? Do you think that word does not exist for me?"

He went on like this for some time, almost shouting. The young man leaned back, and finally interrupted.

"I'm sorry," he said. "I didn't mean to hurt your feelings. And if you allow me, doctor, to tell you in a few words" why he had become a Nazi. He said his mother had lost all her savings with the inflation, and that he, having graduated as a lawyer, could find no work.

Richard posing for Otto

"Since the Führer arrived, I sit at this desk, and for the first time I am making a decent enough living for my mother and me. Before I could not have dreamed of such a thing. Why all of a sudden is it possible?"

In a nutshell, Richard wrote, "I had to leave my mother so that he might be able to support his mother. An Austrian Nazi! Quite unable to see the seriousness of the situation, short-sighted, selfish, unscrupulous, and yet almost disarming in his naivety."

During this time, innumerable Viennese Jews were brutalised or committed suicide. A cousin was struck in the face by crowds, left bleeding, his daughter forced to scrub the pavements with acid in a pail of water.

The British journalist George Gedye commented in his book *Fallen Bastion*: "It is quite impossible to convey to anyone outside Austria in how matter-of-fact a way the Jews of Austria refer to this way (suicide) out of their agony. When I say one's Jewish friends spoke to one of their intention to commit suicide with no more emotion than they had formerly talked of making an hour's journey by train, I cannot expect to be believed."

For those unable to flee and with no means of livelihood, the most likely outcome was death in Dachau concentration camp. According to one Austrian historian, 20 people a day committed suicide in Vienna in the week following the Anschluss and Hitler's triumphal entrance, while other sources put the figure at 1,700 suicides that week, and a total of 7,000 by 1938.

The sales of poisons such as cyanide shot up within days of the Nazis' arrival. In my own family, two close relatives took their lives. They were Arthur's brother Ferry in Brno, who jumped to his death from a cliff, and a giggly cousin called Ilse who had started the leather shop in Vienna with Emma and who threw herself out of a window in Trieste.

Richard arranged for a gentile colleague to take over his most important legal client, a typewriter factory, on condition he pay Josefine a small monthly stipend. The promise was kept only once. He spent his last fortnight sleeping at different friends' houses every night, until thanks to a Nazi official at Thomas Cook he finally obtained a passport stamped with an exit visa. Then followed the frenzied race to get visas to the three countries he had to cross. His first destination was Brno, where he arrived on June 30. "The next morning, at 7 o'clock, three Gestapo men rang the bell of my former office and were told that I had left Austria the day before."

Richard spent ten days in Czechoslovakia, first with his brother Bruno, then in Prague with his sister Klara. He told them they should flee, as the Germans would soon annex Czechoslovakia. "I warned them. The reply I got was, 'That cannot happen here. Our army would fight. 'And who will conquer whom?' I asked, to which they replied, 'Even if the Germans were to be victorious, the Czechs aren't Austrians. They would never do what the Austrians did. Even if conquered, this will remain our country, won't it?'" From Prague, Richard flew to Brussels where he stayed with Emma and Arthur.

For her own safety, Richard had not told his mother of his plans to leave Vienna. But no one had any idea, he later wrote, that Nazi persecution would be so pitiless. Josefine's neighbours in the Wintergasse did not attack or insult her, and Emma sent her money, but Josefine must have felt very alone and scared. She had undoubtedly witnessed outrages, and perhaps too she thought that dying would liberate her children from concerns about her.

In late 1938, she took a kitchen knife and stabbed herself in the stomach. The maid found her so she was taken to hospital, operated on and saved. She had witnessed Kristallnacht on November 10, after which the SA, the SS and ordinary citizens torched synagogues and prayer houses, vandalised shops and businesses owned by Jews, and beat and killed people.

In Bob's eyes, the first sign that the father he had revered was no longer omnipotent was the evening Arthur meekly handed over the keys of his Steyr 200 to the SA who banged on the front door. Many years later, when I gave Bob *The Lost*, Daniel Mendelssohn's book about an American's long search for his Jewish family in Ukraine, he asked me not to be offended if he didn't read it. He had always refused to visit Auschwitz. "It would make me too angry," he said, "and I can't live with that anger."

-22-

1938: The butterfly boy

Bus had been a puny boy, small for his age and quickly out of breath. At his primary school in Brno, he was bullied by budding Nazi classmates, who called him "shrimp", and "typical Jew-boy." But by the age of 17 he was one of Czechoslovakia's best swimmers and was preparing to take part in the 1936 Olympic Games in Berlin. Of the ten boy cousins in my family, Bus was the only serious sportsman.

In the late 19th century, the physician and social critic Max Nordau who with Theodor Herzl co-founded Zionism coined the term *Muskeljudentum* (muscular Judaism), encouraging young Jews to get out into the fresh air and develop their bodies, not just their intellects. Among others, he inspired the founders of Hakoah Vienna, a sports clubs with a top-notch football team that travelled the world, with fans as far as Russia and the United States.

Jewish gold medallists in the former Austro-Hungarian countries were ubiquitous in most sports from tennis, rowing and fencing to wrestling and water polo. In liberal Czechoslovakia, the Maccabi association, an umbrella Zionist organisation, had dozens of sports clubs and received government funding. Hagibor Prague sports association was renowned for its swimmers.

Bus joined Hagibor almost by chance. After his parents had moved from Brno to Prague to open a new Graumann shoe shop there, they allowed him to quit school at 14 to pursue his studies on his own. He did this, spending hours in Prague's main library. At the same time he frequented the sports stadium quite assiduously.

"It was a cold September day, and I felt chilly and miserable as I stepped out of the changing booth in my shorts and vest. It had started to rain. 'What on earth am I doing here?' I said to a boy standing there. 'I'm not good at this, and I'm freezing. What's the point?' He smiled and said, 'I feel exactly the same. I tell you what: can you swim?' I said yes. 'Well why don't you join Hagibor, the Jewish swimming club? It's indoors and it's warm."

His mother Klara had taught Bus to swim in the Danube as a child and in the winter under the wrought-iron dome of Vienna's Dianabad baths. That summer Bus thrashed happily up and down the pool, but the following year he came to the attention of the club's trainers when he beat the country's junior champion. Frantisek Getreuer, nicknamed Getre, was a star, a dashing polyglot who had won all the national freestyle records, as well as a European one. He took Bus under his wing, making him work several hours a day for the Prague senior championships.

At first Bus did not live up to his initial promise, but he was determined to persevere. "I had half drunk the Vltava I swallowed so much water. All my muscles ached and my shoulders were so painful I walked with a stoop. 'All right,' I thought. 'I was rotten at school, and hopeless at athletics. But I can swim."

On the day of the championships, his parents were in the stands. "Sitting among the seniors, nearly all at least five years older than I, I looked like a child. 'You are supposed to compete with these grownups?' my father said with concern. 'Of course, and I'll beat them!,' I said. And beat them I did. This time I was the best breaststroke swimmer in Prague."

While training in the countryside near Brno, Bus observed two Danish girl athletes, the free-style swimmer Ragnhild Hveger and a 12-year-old breaststroke talent, Inge Soerensen who swam 200 metres at a full sprint, and then jumped effortlessly out of the water and started to play around with a football. Soerensen was later to become a symbol of the Danish resistance against the Nazi occupiers.

"I had never seen anything like it and nor had anyone else. The accepted way to swim 200 metres was to do the first 150 metres at a medium pace, and to go into a sprint over the last 50 metres or less." Bus asked Soerensen's coach for her times, but he wouldn't tell. He tried to time her himself with his stopwatch, but was chased away.

"All I knew was that she swam a good deal faster than I did. If this twelve-year-old can do it, so can I, I decided, and started to swim like she did. It was difficult to keep up a full sprint over such a distance, but I could see that it could be done, and eventually I did it, improving my time considerably."

Hitler's Propaganda Minister Joseph Goebbels saw the Berlin Olympics as a golden opportunity. Only months after Germany had passed the Nuremberg laws stripping Jews of their basic rights, discriminatory measures were ostensibly put on hold. The Czech Olympic swimming team was almost entirely made up of Jews, either members of Prague's Hagibor or Bratislava's Jewish swimming club, Bar Kocha Bratislava, and they announced that they wouldn't attend.

Infuriated by this decision, the Czech sports federation disqualified the swimmers from competition for a year, until a number of Czech actors and the writer Max Brod successfully campaigned for the ban to be lifted in time for the 1937 state championships. Bus was on holiday in Ljubljana, but rushed back to Prague on hearing that he could race. Leaping off a tram minutes before the start, he ripped off his clothes, pulled on his swimsuit and jumped into the water - and won.

Bus went on scooping up prizes, but Hitler had been fomenting discontent among Czechoslovakia's Sudetenland majority German-speakers and was now threatening Czechoslovakia. The mountainous regions where the ethnic Germans lived on the edge of Czechoslovakia had been hard hit by the economic crisis, and people there were easy prey for populist rabble-rousing. The mood in Prague was one of resistance. Hagibor sent all its swimmers a letter asking them to cooperate with the police in any voluntary work that might be required of them.

Bus on one of his last walks in Prague

In the middle of the night of May 21, 1938, Klara

woke Bus to tell him to go to the police station. "There had been lots of rumours about a German invasion. We had had practice blackouts, and army searchlights scanned the sky at night." Bus and a handful of other boys waited for hours in a room until at day break they heard the roar of tanks starting their engines and rolling noisily away followed by a long convoy of trucks carrying soldiers. The streets were thronged with soldiers and armed police.

The government had called for total mobilisation, and overnight thousands of soldiers and civilians on the reserve lists had reported with remarkable speed and efficiency to their units or the nearest barracks and from there to their border defences. A sergeant marched Bus to a crossroads beneath Prague's Hradcany castle, and told him to direct the traffic. "It was clear to me now. I was doing an important job, relieving the police so they could join the army on the German border. It was going to be a good day after all. It was to be the last good day."

The army soon returned from the borders with their guns draped in black cloth, looking tired and defeated. The Germans had withdrawn. Bus resumed his training routine, swimming up and down arms only, then alternating short sprints with medium-paced breaststroke. At home, he and his parents listened to the news. "News in Czech, news from Germany, Britain, France. We knew there was going to be war, we wanted to know when."

It was then that he first learned about the fickleness of fear. "I found out, as I did later during the war, that people can't be afraid for very long. A few can't stand the strain and break down or commit suicide, but most get used to it quite quickly and sublimate their fears."

According to Bus, his parents and he had been close to emigrating to Bolivia. So they had considered leaving after all. The landlocked Andean country was among the few that offered asylum to many thousands of refugees, taking in some 20,000 Jews, as told in the book *Hotel Bolivia*. They had filled in forms and were waiting for the visas to arrive when their plans were dashed; the diplomat in charge of visas was sacked on his way back from La Paz while on board a ship crossing to France, and had thrown his papers overboard. After this attempt to stay together as a family, Fritz and Klara concentrated all their efforts on getting their only child to safety.

Under the firm hand of President Edvard Benes, the summer of 1938 was to see Czechoslovakia's last stand against the Nazis. The country's Balkan mountains offered a bastion against Germany's spread to the east, and its fortresses, started in 1936 with help from the French constructors of the Maginot line, were almost impregnable. The country also had a powerful armaments and munitions industry, supplying the British and others with the famous Bren heavy submachine guns. Its tanks and its airforce were among Europe's most modern and effective.

But the Germans continued their campaign of disruption in the Sudeten areas, and the Allies abandoned their promise to defend Czechoslovakia against German aggression. In his Nuremberg speech of September 12, 1938, Hitler hurled insults at Benes's government, inciting the Nazis to revolt in the Sudetenland, which they did, smashing and plundering Jewish property. Geyde from the London *Times* drove to Karlsbad and saw the swastikas, the glass and the debris. The Graumanns had a shoe shop in Karlsbad, and it wasn't spared.

Hitler had warned the Czechs that if they did not hand over the Sudetenland by October 1, 1938, the German army would take it by force. On September 23, Czechoslovakia mobilised again, its reservists racing to the front. "The Czechs were really not afraid to face tremendous odds in defence of their liberties," wrote Gedye. "This was perhaps because they had real liberties to fight for. The republic of Masaryk and Benes was a real democracy, and every individual knew quite clearly for what he was going to stake his life."

Soon after Bus beat the Czechoslovak record for 400-metre breaststroke, the swimming club's secretary handed him a letter from the Maccabi club in London. "They were holding a swimming gala at Goulston Street baths in London's East End. The letter was an invitation to attend and to demonstrate the new butterfly stroke."

From that moment in September 1938, everything happened quickly. The Czech national bank issued Bus with £1 sterling, which was all that was allowed, and Klara bought him a gold ring and a Swiss Schaffhausen gold watch. His passport was renewed, and because they didn't have time to get a picture taken, they used one of his cousin John.

"The most important thing was the suitcase. It had to contain enough clothes to last me a while, since I was hoping to stay illegally in Britain. I didn't have permission to emigrate, not even to visit. The immigration authorities in Britain would decide how long I could stay. Hence the problem with the suitcase: too many clothes would look suspicious. So, one fairly large case with half a dozen shirts and two suits, two pairs of shoes, some underwear, my swimming costumes, and my albums and press cuttings."

For a while, life carried on as normal. Bus went

for early morning training, then to the Graumann shop at the end of Prikopy overlooking St Wenceslas Square, lunch and more training at the military pool in the Vltava, then back to the shop until 7pm. Before he knew it, the train was pulling out of the Wilson station in Prague, and he was leaning out the window. "My mother stood on the platform, waving and smiling. It was 10 am on the 27th of September, a cold sunny day. She was wearing a brown cloth coat with fur trimmings, a shapeless brown hat and felt boots with rubber soles. I knew at that moment that I would never see her again."

When Bus reached Calais, a British ferryboat was waiting in the harbour. "There was nowhere to sit, the boat was very crowded. As soon as it pulled out, an announcement over the loudspeakers called on all foreign nationals to assemble on deck for immigration clearance. There was a long queue, and we advanced slowly, carrying our suitcases. Each passenger or married couple was called one at a time into a small office. It seemed to take hours. In front of me was a Jewish woman in a very emotional state. She was called in, and after a few minutes, she reappeared, crying. She would have to return on the same boat to Germany."

Then came Bus's turn. "I produced my passport. 'Purpose of visit?' 'I have been invited to swim at a gala in London.' 'How do we know you can swim?' the immigration officer asked, rather pleasantly. 'You can see in my album, there are press cuttings.' 'If you are such a good swimmer, why are you so pale? You're not sea sick by any chance?' - again it sounded like a joke, but there was a searching look in his eyes.

"'I am a bit, actually. A swimming pool doesn't have waves.' He put a large rubber stamp in my passport and laughed, 'OK. I'll believe you. Three weeks. Just three weeks. OK?" Bus hadn't been seasick but he was weak with hunger. Now he was heading for London. The other swimmers of Prague's Hagibor club were not so lucky. When the time came to consider emigration, the swimming champion Getreuer stayed in Prague because he had a mentally disabled brother he refused to leave behind. They were both murdered in concentration camps, as were nearly all the club's 300 members. Bus never swam competitively again.

On September 29, two days after Bus's train drew out of the Wilson station, the Sudetenland areas were handed over to Hitler at the Munich peace conference with the consent of Britain, France and Italy. British and French diplomats then conveyed messages from their governments telling President Benes that if he did not comply Czechoslovakia would be blamed for German aggression. The government chose to surrender rather than trigger a hopeless war.

"As the news of the surrender came," wrote Gedye, "a nation broke into tears. You saw them literally at every corner, in every doorway, in every café, men and women, their eyes red with tears of shame and rage." If Bus's parents Fritz and Klara cried too, they must also have shed tears of relief that their son had left the country.

-23-

1938: The fragility of privilege

B russels is where my sister Lucy and I have lived almost all our adult lives. The Catholic school my father briefly attended in St Boniface still exists today. The Cambre Abbey, where my grandparents celebrated their Catholic wedding, is a favourite spot to show to visiting friends. As Bob was to discover when he came up from Paris many years later, the apartment his parents had rented in Brussels in 1938 was in Rue des Champs Elysées, the same street that by coincidence I was then living in. His brother John had found it, having arrived in Brussels ahead of Emma and Bob, joining a "lonely and preoccupied" Arthur.

Shortly after Bob arrived, the brothers went to see Walt Disney's *Snow White* in a huge American-style movie house with a theatre organ that rose up through the floor. Brussels felt opulent in those days where money from the Belgian Congo had gone into the building of monuments and private houses. They walked in the city's surrounding beech forest and spoke in Viennese dialect for fun. More importantly, Emma set to work to obtain transit visas through Brussels for her brothers Richard and Bruno.

Richard's arrest in Vienna was likely any day, but Belgian consulates were issuing transit visas only to people who had an entry visa to another country. The brothers were hoping to reach London, and so needed guarantees from Otto who was already there. But old rancours must have smarted, and Emma had to repeatedly galvanise her brother into action for the papers to be secured.

The apartment in Brussels was soon cramped. Richard arrived and stayed for a month, as did Bruno who was trying to get his wife and two sons out of Czechoslovakia. John, now 18, had to be moved away if the rooms were not to explode with the tensions. Arthur sent him to London with the stern injunction that he must decide for himself what to study there. A bank account with a generous sum of money on it awaited him. "Father was well informed and his predictions so far had been correct," wrote John. "Mother expressed anxiety at my ineptitude to look after my own affairs."

The day after John reached London in mid-September, Prime Minister Neville Chamberlain flew to Germany to meet Hitler, and two weeks later the Munich agreement heralded the dismantlement of Czechoslovakia. John felt the world had become insane and that his own sanity was under threat.

Although he had always admired England, Richard would have preferred exile in the softer Italian climes he knew well from having holidayed there. But after a rough ferry journey from Ostend, and a long interrogation by immigration officials, he was greatly moved by an act of kindness he came to see as typically English. It was cold and raining, and he felt lonely and exhausted. When waiting for the train to London, an elderly English porter with a massive white moustache sat on the bench next to him.

"He told me not to worry. The English, he said, are friendly people if you only came to know them a little. They are helpful to oppressed people and don't bother about where you came from. They would help me too, as I would find out." The man talked with Richard for an hour and a half, finally helping him into his compartment and taking just one coin from the handful of small change Richard extended.

In Brussels, Arthur was receiving letters from relatives addressed to 'Herr Konsul' pleading for help. He represented a beacon of hope, but there was little he could do; too many people needed him. Bob remembered meeting a young man from Emma's side of the family. He was a hairdresser by trade, ruddy-faced and uneducated, who had crossed the German border illegally into Belgium at night, and was surviving in hiding as best he could. "It took a split second for Emma to bring him to our *pension* and to set him to work cutting Arthur's and my hair."

Bob, who was 13, was polite but bemused. "This boy was a Jew, a real one. He looked different, he spoke with an accent, he used words I didn't know, and gestures ridiculed in our circles. Moreover, he was a proletarian. The question arose, was I one of them? He had lived in a world where people studied little, ate heavy food, told clumsy stories, suffered persistent and overt anti-semitism, and were used to it."

"I was a willing victim to his scissors, and glad to see Emma slipping him some money, but I felt invulnerable, which I am sure he did not. There is not much to add to the story. It was just an encounter between a protected, Catholic Austrian boy - with a recently discovered Jewish ancestry - and a Viennese Jewish working class boy. Except that we were related."

Music and classical culture had been central to Bob's upbringing, and meeting this relative - just a few years older than he - would have evoked the impermanence of privilege, reminding him that his family had not long been settled into the middle class. Both Bob and John must have felt that their past sense of entitlement had been but a thin veneer, their working class and Jewish origins but a breath away.

The intellectual and impractical John didn't feel any more proletarian than he felt Jewish. Rather he saw himself as the product of a "baroque" education, one of classical learning about ideas and values that had no practical content. He had arrived in London, and found the English unfathomable. For a while he lived in the upstairs bedroom of his uncle Otto's and aunt Hilde's house, paying them rent. He listened to their tips for living successfully as refugees in London, ie "nothing in one's stance, movement or dress must ever betray one as a continental. To be rated as 'charming' was to be socially acceptable."

I don't believe Otto saw the arrival of his brothers and nephews with a welcoming eye. Hilde and he had left an increasingly violent Vienna with relief, but in London they were barely self-supporting. They had just acquired a lease on a cottage in St Johns Wood, with its own studio at the back. When Richard arrived, he had moved into the tiny apartment they had just vacated, but they rowed after his first visit to the artists' cottage and stopped seeing each other.

Bruno, the eldest of the three Flatter brothers, and the most central European in appearance with his aquiline nose and black eyes, and in temperament with his flamboyant personality, was the next to arrive from Brussels. He took lodgings in a room across the street from Richard. When he visited Otto, he told him off for rejecting their brother, and left the house in a huff.

You would think that despite the financial strain they were all under, exacerbated by the fact that money could no longer be taken out of Austria or Czechoslovakia, the brothers might have remembered their father's death-bed injunction about family unity. But instead the tensions were now in high relief, and the circumstances put such pressure on each of them that they became obsessed with their own problems.

Bus had always been like a brother to John, but the newly London-based John was immature and although he knew that in Prague Bus was in danger, he was ineffective and naive. A particularly sad incident reveals his confusion about what it meant to be a Jew. He went to the British Committee for Refugees from Czechoslovakia in Mecklenburgh Square, without knowing that it had been started by London Jews to save Jews. "It was a pity I did not know. As my turn came in the long queue and I told the lady that I had a cousin in Prague, she looked me straight in the eyes and asked, 'Is he a Jew?'"

John confusedly replied something about Nazi laws, and that perhaps Bus wasn't really quite Jewish. "She snapped, 'We are terribly busy now helping Jews, and I am sorry, but we cannot afford to waste time on people who are not really Jews. Next please!' I went out into the street and cried bitterly. It was the most shameful moment in my life, and for decades I could not mention it to anyone."

In Vienna before his exile John had been looking

forward to adulthood. He was studying compulsively and his eating disorders were in abeyance, as was his rage against his mother and the world at large. But in London he lacked his father's advice about what to do, how to behave, what to think. He felt guilty that compared to his relatives he was well off. "I would have done anything to save Bus, my brother since my playpen. Yet I felt ashamed of a treasonable lack of solidarity with the Jewish cause."

In the end, it was Richard who came up with the solution. It was he who asked the Maccabi swimming club to apply for a short-stay visa for Bus so that he could display the butterfly stroke. This is John's explanation, which differs from Bus's but is the one I believe. Different memoirs tell the same story differently because memory plays tricks, and also because emotions distort facts. Whatever the truth, no one in Bus's mind had done enough to save his parents.

When Bus arrived that September 1938 in London, aged 18, with only £1 in his pocket, Richard was the first of the three uncles he went to visit. "I found him in lodgings in St Johns Wood, one room and a small, messy kitchen. He was wearing a blanket over his clothes, and looked pathetic. Greeting me in his schoolmasterly manner, he offered me some bread and cheese and produced a cup of tea with great ceremoniousness and much difficulty."

Then he told Bus to look for work, and as Bus was in awe of him, he left determined to be worthy of his uncle. His parents trapped in Prague were always on his mind, and he thought obsessively about how to get them out. "I found out there was a way. My father could leave if someone were to put £50 into a special account as a guarantee, and my mother could come as a domestic servant. I knew she wouldn't have minded being a servant, but that she would not come without my father." The £50 turned out to be way out of his reach.

Bruno and his family in Karlsbad enjoying the last days of insouciance

In broken English, Bruno was devoting his considerable energies to establishing a business in London. Friends of Richard's had lent Bruno the money to get his wife and two boys out of Czechoslovakia. After trying to market industrial varnish from Czechoslovakia, and then leather dye, he set up a small factory for the recovery and reuse of waste materials. The impractical John was sent to slash the leather from old cars to use for leather dyeing demonstrations, and Richard helped by using his Shakespearean English to write business letters.

While John studied English so he could sit his matriculation exam for the London School of Economics, Bus worked briefly in a shoe shop, which allowed him to apply for a permit to stay in England. He learned English on the hoof, whereas John's approach was to exert such mental discipline as to banish all German thoughts from his mind, even while day-dreaming. "I cut the moorings from my mother tongue," he wrote. "My dislike of German became so intense that for many years I could speak it only haltingly, in a dialect or with a distorting accent."

In late 1939, Solvay opened a Zurich office as its East European headquarters, just a room and a couple of desks, as a good place for fund repatriation. John was devastated when he heard that Arthur was going there. Brussels seemed close enough to London, but Zurich felt unreachable. In adolescence, John has grown intellectually very close to his father, almost too close as he believed he needed Arthur's advice for almost every step he took.

Emma's first concern was to move her mother Josefine out of Vienna to Zurich, but there were endless hurdles even for a frail old woman. Josefine owned her house, and the Nazis wanted tax payments and many forms to be filled in before they would let her go. Almost a year went by before my great-grandmother finally reached Zurich. She was in poor health and profoundly desperate, although she gamely paraphrased Goethe, saying "Movement is life, stillness is death." She died soon afterwards, aged 75, and her ashes were buried there by a lake. I have a picture of her lonely graveyard plaque.

In London, Bus didn't know who to approach for the £50 guarantee needed for his father. The people at the Czechoslovak Refugee Trust Fund, as the committee for Czech refugees was now called, were dismissive. He'd heard that the Quakers might be helpful, but he couldn't gather up the courage to enter their imposing building opposite Euston Station. "It is difficult nowadays to understand why I didn't make a more determined effort to get hold of a sponsor. In those days the generation gap was infinitely greater, and no one took my fears for my parents' lives seriously."

Then as now, refugees were seen as a threat to national security, so when Britain declared war on Germany on September 3, 1939, the British started to see Fifth Columnists crawling out of the woodwork everywhere. Richard and Otto were virulently anti-Nazi, yet they were also Austrians and thus on the enemy side. Both were called before a special tribunal in London set up to assess potential enemy spies, and like many Jews were classed C - no security risk.

But after the fall of France in June 1940, in the weeks when the German army moved to occupy France's Channel and Atlantic coasts, the British rounded up 27,000 German, Austrian and Italian men and some women. The mood had changed and spies were being seen all over the place as fears of a German invasion grew. Bricks were thrown into the windows of German-owned shops. Winston Churchill famously said "Collar the lot". Both brothers were reclassified as enemy aliens.

Some of these men were sent to camps set up on race courses and unfinished housing estates, but most were ordered to the Isle of Man which had been used for internment during the First World War. Richard, who was close to 50, was among those transported to Commonwealth countries following an agreement reached in July 1940. He was lucky not to have been among the 7,000 men deported from Liverpool to Canada on the Arandora Star, the liner torpedoed off the Irish coast by a German submarine. It sank in 35 minutes, drowning its 800 passengers. His own journey was to nevertheless become one of Britain's most embarrassing wartime scandals.

-24-

1942: Fifth columnists

A week after the sinking of the Arandora Star, 2,542 German, Austrian and Italian men considered too risky to stay on British shores - Richard among them - were shipped from Liverpool to Australia on HMT Dunera, a troop carrier designed to carry half that number. They weren't told where they were headed, not even once on board. As well as 2,036 mostly Jewish anti-Nazis were a few hundred German prisoners of war, Nazi sympathisers and Italian fascists.

The Dunera, before its days as a prison on the ocean

Doctors, lawyers, musicians, artists, art historians, photographers, physicists, rabbis, labourers and Sigmund Freud's grandson Walter were guarded by 300 ill-trained British guards, seven officers from the newly formed Royal Pioneer Corps, one medical officer and the ship's crew. The guards believed their prisoners to be Nazi spies and saboteurs, and confiscated their luggage, helped themselves to the contents of their wallets, and tore up their documents or threw them overboard. This set the tone for the journey.

During the entire 57-day voyage, the deportees were held below deck with hatches and portholes tightly closed, in almost total darkness. They slept close together in hammocks, on benches, a table or on the floor, using their boots as pillows. For half an hour a day, they were allowed on deck and marched around in single file, watched over by guards with fixed bayonets and machine-guns trained on them. The guards shouted and beat them, and were allowed to do so by their commander, Lt-Col William Patrick Scott.

Water was strictly rationed and there were maggots in the food. Three men died, one of them jumping overboard. The best off were those who had some contact with the more compassionate crew. "We were unshaven – we were forbidden to shave – and we were not allowed to put our hands in our pockets," Richard wrote. "For a fortnight we had to come on deck barefoot, my shirt had to do duty day and night for the whole two months and was in rags before long – not one of us was allowed to get at his suitcase – why all this was, nobody knew, nobody could tell us."

Richard remembered a handsome 17-year-old Jewish boy "with bright eyes and a bitter mouth" who came from Swabia in central Germany. "He was small but strong and lively and there was an impish smile around his eyes. He had a slight limp. One day I asked him about it and he told me his story. That was bad enough, but the more terrible thing was the casual way he told it."

The boy's father had died in a concentration camp, his grandmother had been burned alive in bed during the Kristallnacht pogroms, and he last saw his mother as she jumped from a window in their apartment. He too jumped, breaking his ankle. He was put in a concentration camp until a children's organisation brought him to England. A farmer hired him to look after his sheep, and then he was arrested and put on the Dunera.

Despite the brutality, the fear and the fatigue, the journey had its tragic-comic moments, like the celebration of Goethe's birthday beneath the overcrowded hatches. Some passengers formed a choir for which they wrote the music from memory on pieces of toilet paper. Richard kept the manuscript of a choir from Bach's *St Matthew Passion* thus transcribed. One day all the prisoners queued up in a long line to glimpse Capetown and the flat-topped Table Mountain through a lavatory porthole.

During those hellish days, Richard had time to ponder what it meant to be a Jew, and sought out one of the rabbis on board. "He was mid-ship near the engines, and one could hardly breathe in the swelter of the low and overcrowded hold. Stripped to the waist as we were sailing through the tropical zone off Africa, we talked while rivulets of sweat ran down our faces and we didn't bother to wipe them off. Our knees touched those of the men sitting opposite, and we had to speak loudly in the general hubbub."

Richard told the rabbi a little about himself, and then asked him if the Jewish faith could be summarised in one sentence. The rabbi replied, "Thou shalt Love the Lord my God with all thy heart and with all thy soul," and "Thy shalt love thy neighbour as thyself."

"As a man who has kept to these commandments as best he could, but has ignored the prayers, rites and ceremonial observances, can I claim be a good Jew?" Richard asked.

"No," said the rabbi. "Man grapples on his own in the dark, and only prayer can keep him in a continuous connection with God."

"Good works aren't enough," the rabbi said. "They can lead to pride and self-satisfaction. A Jew must follow the faith of his fathers."

I can well imagine the crammed bodies, the forced intimacy, the sweat, the sound of the water crashing against the ship's hull.

They spoke for more than an hour before Richard got up and thanked him. "Come and speak to me again, I am always happy to discuss issues of faith." But Richard didn't return because he felt that though they had breathed the same air, oceans and continents kept them apart.

The deportees were held below deck when they docked successively in Sierra Leone, Ghana, South Africa, and finally Freemantle, the first Australian port. From there the Dunera sailed on to Melbourne, where it disembarked a few dozen men, before finally reaching Sydney. A journalist described the internees as "slinking rat-faced men", and the ship's commander was welcomed with open arms.

The first medical officer to board the ship was shocked. The men were filthy, bedraggled, sometimes ill and most of them in lamentable physical and psychological condition. His damning report eventually led to a court martial for Scott and two other officers, although it was so hush-hush that the internees were not called on to testify. The court martial was later described as a cover-up, and the details of the Dunera affair are still protected by the Official Secrets Act.

Richard and his fellow prisoners were put on a train for New South Wales's Hay Internment Camp, which was not fully built yet. On Australia's dry, windswept east coast, an 18-hour train journey from Sydney, this was one of the eight larger internment camps in Australia where the men were treated like prisoners of war.

"I was taken by ambulance to the nearest hospital, where a soldier sat beside me, a rifle between his knees, and a bayonet on his rifle. In hospital, three soldiers kept watch over me night and day, taking turns of eight hours each, sitting on a chair near my bed. Every time I was x-rayed, a soldier followed the wheelchair into the x-ray room. When in pyjamas, dressing gown and slippers, I went to the lavatory, the soldier followed me along the ward where all the patients would stare."

He tried to explain his situation to the nurses, but they didn't believe him. "'But surely,' one of them said frankly, 'you must have done something wrong, or why should they have sent you all the way to Australia?'"

The Hay camp was built on treeless grazing land for sheep, regularly swept by sand storms; the men were housed in wooden huts in three compounds, and slept like soldiers on straw paillasses. But the food and sanitary conditions were four-star compared to those on the ship. Within a few weeks they had made the camp liveable; they organised classes, concerts, plays, set up a football team and named it Juventus Turin, after their favourite Italian team, and even created their own currency. They got support from the Quakers, who brought books and established a link with Melbourne University that allowed people to sit exams.

Richard taught, like the handful of other former teachers and professors. He found it difficult to work on his own writing and translations with so many men constantly around him, but did write a new play and translate *The Winter's Tale*, concluding like Alexander Pope that it had not been penned by Shakespeare, although that theory now seems disproved.

In the hut he shared with 20 men, Richard chalked up a quotation from *Hamlet*:

There's a divinity that shapes our ends,
Rough-hew them how we will

Whenever the inscription began to fade, he would write it out again. He must have seen it as meaning that his fate was in the hands of a higher purpose, but also that fate contained a measure of free will.

In Britain, the House of Commons had begun to react to the arbitrary internments, and the first prisoners were released quite quickly. The Australian authorities were informed that Richard had been an active anti-Nazi, but it took 18 months before he was escorted to a ship returning to England. In London, he was quickly admitted to Saint Bartholomew's Hospital - Bart's – with what must have been tuberculosis or some other lung affection. His odyssey was over.

Otto's internment in that summer of 1940 did not take him as far and was not nearly as dramatic, but he never entirely forgave the British for his humiliation. He and his family had always been ardent anglophiles who looked to England as a model of civilisation, but in July two police officers appeared at his studio door saying they had orders to take him into custody.

"Looking at the drawing I had been working on, they remarked that they had never arrested an artist before. My wife came to the studio. The officers asked her to pack a few things for me, 'just enough for a weekend trip', they said, I was not to be held for long."

Otto was to spend three months in "Camp M" on the Isle of Man, a few hours ferry ride from Liverpool, in a row of Victorian guest houses surrounded by barbed wire. There were several camps on the island, including one for women and children. With him were German artisans, clerks and waiters, but mostly refugees from Germany and Austria of different ages, social classes and political opinion.

"Strangers confronted one another in bewilderment. There were the timid ones who already saw themselves being strung up by the invading German soldiers, the rumour-mongers who spread sinister tales, a few Nazi sympathisers who expressed their hope of a speedy liberation by the German army but who became more and more subdued as time went on and the invasion failed to materialise."

Each house had its own rations for the week, although internees were allowed food parcels and letters. "The incompatibles formed a society. University teachers lectured, doctors and dentists treated patients, young men prepared themselves for examinations, others underwent re-training for work in the countries they planned to emigrate to after the war. I gave some drawing lessons but my main occupation was cooking. The seclusion of the kitchen is not unlike that of an artist's studio." Hilde visited three times, talking to Otto through the barbed wire fence. She was using all her contacts to secure his release.

Two men helped Otto cook for the 80 inmates in his house. One of these was a German-born miner who had always lived in Scotland but had not bothered to get himself naturalised, preferring to spend his money on drink. He felt Scottish and didn't speak any German. "I became attached to several men of admirable character, but we lost touch after our release. They and I probably did not want to be reminded of those days of impotence and disgrace." The day a guard called out his name, "how beautiful my name sounded then. I was a free man again."

A few days after he got home to St Johns Wood's cottage in Elm Tree Road, the telephone rang; it was the police asking him to stay in for a call from the Ministry of Information. The call came and an official invited him to their office, but Otto was so nervous that he didn't think of asking for the address. "I, the enemy alien, did not dare to ask over the phone where the ministry building was." It was near Russell Square, and when he got there he was asked if he would submit cartoons intended for German soldiers preparing to invade England.

"The official impressed on me that this meant highly secret work, that I was not to talk about it or show my sketches to anyone, not even to my wife. He said that at night I would have to keep the drawings in a sealed portfolio by my bedside."

Thus, Otto concluded, he had risen almost overnight from enemy alien to officially sanctioned conspirator in secret work. His manhood was restored, and he learned later that Lord Vansittart, then chief adviser at the Foreign Office and an early anti-Hitlerian, had seen his satirical cartoons and acted as his sponsor. Otto spent the rest of the war drawing propaganda for the Ministry of Information.

During his uncles' internment, John was fighting his own demons. Compared to relatives in London and back home in Austria and Czechoslovakia, he felt unfairly privileged. He couldn't do what his father wanted, to get on with his studies. His mind simply wasn't on them.

"To make things worse, Arthur's brother-in-law my uncle Edgar sent me a letter asking me if I could get him the addresses of insurance people of his rank in England." He apparently hoped that one of them might help his two sons leave Czechoslovakia. John went to the Chamber of Commerce, and copied a random list of names. He couldn't think of anything better to do. His cousins were to be among the many Czech relatives to perish.

Unhappy and disconsolate, John and Bus shared a cheap room in Swiss Cottage near Hampstead for a while, and became increasingly irritable with each other. Bus had returned to London after a spell as a labourer on a Staffordshire farm in the Midlands where he was ruthlessly exploited. John became obsessed with the fact that he had a German name, signed up to join the Czechoslovakian army in exile, but didn't report when called up. He feared he was a deserter.

The Czechoslovak Army was an undermanned armoured brigade within the British Army, made up of young refugees with Czech passports. When Bus received his call-up papers, he travelled to Leamington Spa in Warwickshire, where various forms had to be filled out.

"A sergeant had one of the forms in his typewriter.
-Name
-Graumann, Ernest
-Born where and when?
-18.12.1919, in Vienna, Austria
-Religion?

-Without religion

-Mother tongue?

-German

-Nationality?

This referred to what would now be called ethnic origin, not to citizenship, and it gave me a moment's thought. Everything so far had made me out to be a German.

-Jew, I said.

That was the first time in my life I had ever said that, or thought that, about myself. I knew perfectly well that I came from an entirely Jewish family, but until Hitler's race laws being a Jew had been a matter of religion. It is interesting that the Nazis' view of Jews as a race has been gradually adopted by the Jews themselves, but that was certainly not something my parents and I or anyone else at the time believed in."

-25-

1940s: Three stops on the way to America

My grandparents naturally hoped for a rapid German defeat once Britain and France had declared war. But eight months later, the Germans invaded Belgium. The Solvay management stayed in Belgian hands, unlike the company's subsidiary in Germany where the Nazis took control, but they were not allowed to have Jewish employees, and nor were they allowed an entirely free hand.

Arthur rented an apartment in Zurich when they arrived in the spring of 1939, and Bob went to a Swiss-German school, where he learned to speak *Switzerdeutsch*. I have a class picture of him with his vigorous dark hair, wearing a suit. After the French front collapsed, and Italy entered the war on the German side in June 1940 check, Switzerland was surrounded by the Axis countries.

Emma was doing everything she could to help friends and family by sending money and acting as a post box to transfer letters from Austria and Czechoslovakia to London and the United States. She put her life at risk by going to Vienna after her mother's suicide attempt, where she nursed her and convinced her that life was still worth living. Arthur was working, but his boss was no longer satisfied, as according to a note in Solvay's archives he complains that Arthur was not in good mental shape.

Of course, my grandfather was better informed than many about events in occupied Czechoslovakia because it was easier to obtain news in neutral Switzerland. He realised that his brothers, his sister and his nephews would have to leave if they were to survive, and that Czechoslovakia, the country he had felt so close to, was now as dangerous for Jews as Vienna had been. In 1941 he decided that the whole family should emigrate to the United States, and resigned from Solvay, agreeing to a modest pension.

He may have found it intolerable to go on working for a company that produced chemicals used by the Germans, but in any case his heart was no longer in his work. His boss was almost relieved to see him go because his anxiety was intolerable, as I learned from some official correspondence I was later to read. He accepted a very small pension because he no doubt assumed that at the age of 52 he would find work in America.

The US Consulate in Zurich turned down his request for visas to the United States, so he bought visas to Cuba instead in the belief that the US Consulate in Havana would be more amenable. Arthur had put money aside, which he now spent on securing American sponsorship for his relatives via a cousin in New York, buying various papers and passages on ships sailing from Lisbon to Cuba. At some point, he must have known he was too late, and realised he had failed his three siblings.

Zurich was the site of an unsettling experience for Bob, the day strangers walked through their rented apartment buying the furniture and possessions he had known since childhood. Gone were the tables, the sideboards and the armchairs. Gone the silverware and paintings. Seeing people casually pick and choose objects that he had always known was yet another indication that nothing was ever permanent.

The Germans had not yet invaded the south of France when the three left Zurich in early 1942, not long after Josefine's death and burial. They boarded a train to Geneva that took them the length of unoccupied France. "We stopped often," Bob wrote. "We saw Red Cross trains carrying wounded soldiers. We drank ersatz coffee at *buffets de la gare* in places like Annecy and Narbonne." In Annecy, they again met the distant relative of Emma who had cut their hair in Brussels, and was waiting for them on the platform.

"He had fled Belgium, God knows how," Bob wrote; "One didn't follow everyone's unbelievable tales in those days. He had worked in a logging camp somewhere in the mountains, and knew of our passage through Annecy. He was wearing a French army uniform, shyly proud of his martial appearance. I was astounded to see him embrace Emma. '*Tante* Emma!' he cried, with an intensity of affection that was not usual in our family. He wished us a good trip to the New World. One can only conjecture how much of his life remained, another two or three years perhaps.

"The logging camp could not have lasted very long if it was subsidised by a Jewish charity. After that there would have been another camp, a transit camp on the way to the east. Or did he escape? Try to escape? When the war was over, Emma never mentioned the young man again. So many had disappeared. He was just one of them. And we hardly knew him."

Arthur had lost his self-confidence and composure, so both parents now relied on 16-year-old Bob to deal with customs men and passport controls. Besides, the French he had learned in Brussels was better than theirs. At the Spanish border, they boarded a bus for Barcelona and then another bus to Madrid. They witnessed the devastation caused by the German bombing raids during the Spanish Civil War.

After a night or two in Madrid, they travelled over the mountains by train to Lisbon and waited for the Portuguese steamer that was to transport them to Cuba. I have a copy of the letter Arthur wrote in September from a Lisbon hotel to his boss Eudore Lefèvre, expressing in French his gratitude for the 20 years spent working by his side.

I discovered it in the archives of Solvay's Brussels headquarters, inside a folder of letters Arthur had written to his former colleagues offering his services, and also mentioning his dwindling pension and ill health, sending his congratulations after the liberation of Brussels. The file contained the bill for the transport of my family's furniture from Klosterneuburg to Brussels, and a tacky Christmas card Arthur later sent from America.

As I studied this sad little collection of papers illustrating my grandfather's fall from professional grace, I drew some comfort from seeing for the first time his clear handwriting on these brave and pathetic missives, a little bit of the real man, like traces of blood. It was clear that the erstwhile highly competent lawyer in Vienna who had travelled far and wide to update Solvay's legal arrangements in the post-Habsburg world was now seen as little more than an irritating person making unrealistic demands.

The sea journey from Portugal to Havana was

meant to have been in first class, but when they embarked, the threesome were directed to a second-class cabin on what was a dirty and badly run ship. Arthur's pride must have slipped several notches. Bob had always said that they weren't really refugees because his father still had money, but it is clear they were very much refugees. During the journey they were stopped by a German submarine that insisted on inspecting the neutral ship's cargo.

A number of surprises met them in Havana. "We weren't allowed ashore," wrote Bob. "Motorboats transported us to barracks on the shore opposite Havana. We had to carry our own luggage in the tropical heat. There we occupied double decker bunks in vast dormitories. We were officially in quarantine, but after several days it became clear that we were going to be milked. My father negotiated a reasonable sum with the Cuban officials." The barracks at Tiscornia were a sort of Ellis Island where the authorities extorted money from refugees before they were allowed to enter Cuba.

Bob was counting the days for the American visas to arrive

Bob's experience of the dictator Batista's Cuba resembles that of historian Peter Gay's, who recalls in his book *My German Question* how the German-speaking refugees formed a community of more than 3,000 where talk was chiefly of friends and family trapped by the Nazis, and what they could do to help them. Cuba had

Sephardic families that had fled persecution in 15th-century Spain, and Ashkenazis who had escaped the pogroms in Russia and Poland. But these people had nothing in common with the latest wave of refugees, most of whom intended to leave as soon as they had received visas for the United States or somewhere in South America.

Cuba was wrestling with a seriously depressed economy. Its record of admitting refugees was among the world's best, even if anti-immigrant demonstrations occurred regularly. The United States only allocated a limited number of monthly slots to Czech and Austrian-born would-be immigrants, and my grandparents soon realised that they were not at the top of the list. Solvay was also thought to be on a black list for aiding the German war industry.

Emma kept house in a rented apartment, shopping at an open market and hiring a domestic help, so they settled into a curious, transient routine. They ate lobster and pineapples every day because these were cheap. They may have gone once or twice to the Reissmann restaurant that served Wiener Schnitzel, Viennese cakes and coffee *mit Schlag*. Arthur kept up a correspondence with John in London about books and philosophy. "We never mentioned New York," wrote John, "and I was encouraged to think that it no longer interested him." Because his parents were permanently preoccupied, Bob dealt with all the practical arrangements.

"For some time in my late childhood and adolescence, I lived in a world of refugees without being one myself - my privileged situation, due to my father's position, income and contacts, gave me a degree of assurance that others did not have," Bob wrote. Most of the refugees the family met in Cuba were depressed, although many kept a sense of humour. A popular joke told of the refugee dachshund that claimed to have been a Saint Bernard in Europe.

"We made friends with Jewish immigrants, academics, doctors and intellectuals reduced to the level of beggars, the women working as maids, and then it really hit me. Conversations were mainly about the past and the difficulty of finding a place that would accept them." Bob learned at first-hand how terrible life had been for other Austrian and German Jews, and the extent of the administrative hurdles the Nazis had created to make them pay all the money they could before even hoping to leave their homes.

"I remember faces," Bob recalled. "A handsome couple of communist doctors. A former judge from Dresden with a wooden leg. A dentist who brought his equipment to Havana and practised his profession illegally. A professor of German who spoke with a Yiddish accent and was a great admirer of Wagner. What made these people so resilient? They must have been the tough ones. The weaker were not able to get out and many committed suicide."

Few of these refugees had the means to support themselves, and relied on assistance from the Jewish Relief Committee, commonly referred to as 'The Joint'". Arthur's small pension stretched quite a way in Havana, although that wasn't going to be the case in America.

Bob attended a British-American high school, and later took courses at the university where Fidel Castro was among his fellow students. He must have been struck by the variety of people's skin colours, all shades of brown, and he enjoyed the sandy beaches and Havana's splendid ice-cream parlours. He loved the jazz music and the brass orchestras, but was impatient to get to New York. His father's mental collapse must have been hard to take, as Bob had once known him as a man admired and respected by all. In Cuba, Arthur learned that his youngest brother Ferry had committed suicide jumping to his death from a rock on the Barrandov, a hill outside Prague.

Eventually hiring a New York lawyer, Arthur and some other refugees found a US Senator who sponsored them against payment. After almost two years, the visas finally came through, and they arrived in Miami where Arthur was questioned for several hours by FBI agents who may have suspected him of being an industrial spy. They also confiscated most of the written material in my grandparents' luggage, including letters, address books and the script for uncle Otto's puppet theatre. I sometimes wonder if there is a vast hall within Miami's immigration buildings full of confiscated property of this kind, memorabilia deemed too dangerous to be left in the hands of their owners. This was when Arthur dropped the extra n from our family name to Americanise it.

-26-

1942: Death in Sobibor

Bus's parents died in 1942 in Poland's Sobibor concentration camp. A photographer had taken their picture two or three years earlier in the streets of Prague. This was among their son's most precious possessions, the last photo of his parents he had. They are wrapped up against the cold and look like any middle-aged couple, their faces closed, no clues as to what they were feeling. Where were they going? What had they done that day? What was on their minds?

Last photograph of Klara and Fritz, a stolen moment in Prague

It is not known whether the many travel documents Arthur had painstakingly assembled in Zurich over weeks and months ever reached his Czech brothers and sister, his sister-in-law and his nephews. But if they did, it was too late. Bus was always convinced more should have been done, and may not have believed his uncle had spent all his savings on those travel documents. Deep down he may well have resented his five surviving cousins for still having their own parents.

On my grandmother Emma's side, only her sister Klara, was murdered. She is remembered as an outgoing and affectionate woman, more comfortable with herself than Emma. They looked alike, but Klara had a softer face and dimples when she smiled.

"My mother had an exceptionally good disposition and a great sense of fun," Bus recalled. He admitted to me that he probably idealised his parents, but only slightly if that was so. "She loved people who had no pretensions, particularly poor people, beggars, street singers, gypsies." Her instincts were always to be on the side of the underdog. She once crossed the street in Vienna because she saw a woman hitting her child, and slapped the woman hard. 'Did you like that?" she shouted. "Well, your child doesn't either!"

Klara liked to say that poor people were rich people with no money, and that education was the leveller. Her socialist convictions probably explained why she didn't get along with her vivacious sister-in-law Ilka, disapproving of her chic villa in Brno, and glamorous holidays spent skiing or on the Italian riviera. The Brno family would tut-tut when Klara went to the market without wearing gloves or a hat, just like a vulgar working woman. One day she told Bus that if he ever wanted to end a relationship with a woman, she knew how to write break-up letters, as she had had plenty of practice doing this for her bother Bruno.

As a baby, Bus had been recorded as "without confession" (*Konfessionloss*) in Vienna's civil register because his parents didn't believe in God. "We read Jewish authors and we had Jewish friends, but we weren't religious," Bus told me at his home outside Cardiff. Only inter-marriage, Klara said, would put an end to anti-semitism. Bus came home from school in Vienna one day with a joke he'd heard about a Jew and a Catholic. Klara was intrigued. "What's a Jew?" she quizzed him. "A *bad* person," Bus replied, repeating what he heard people around him say.

Like Emma, Klara disapproved of vanity and dressed plainly. By their mid-thirties, both women looked somewhat dumpy. Bus remembered going with his mother to a hat shop. She pointed at a shapeless brown model on display, put it on her head to see if it fitted and paid. A hat, she said, was simply meant to keep your head warm. In her youth, she had learned to knit and crochet, and did this with skill. But she always gave away the tablecloths she had decorated with elaborate animal and flower patterns because she disliked owning anything fussy.

A keen reader of fiction and books on psychology, Klara was interested in children and education. She had a soothing effect on John, and Bob felt she listened to him, which wasn't always the case in his own home. When Bus, aged 14, told his parents that he wanted to stop school, neither of them protested. Their views were too liberal to oppose him. Instead, they advised him to visit Prague's library to continue learning, when he wasn't helping his father in the shoe shop. Other family members were shocked at their laissez faire approach.

"I soon believed that this had been a mistake," Bus wrote, "and that they had treated me as an adult too soon. They shouldn't have given in to me on so many matters, like my schooling. But not much later, alone in London, I realised that my parents had in fact taught me to think clearly, to make my own decisions and to take the consequences for my actions."

In faded sepia snapshots and more professional portraits by studio photographers, Klara's husband Fritz is slender with timid eyebrows, small round glasses, and what was thought to be an English moustache. When he left the house, he'd tap his hat twice to say 'I'm off'. In the shoe shop, the customers called him "doctor" for his attentive manner. Klara may have been defiantly indifferent to fashion, but Fritz was dapper and neatly turned out. His shoes were beautifully maintained, and Bus claimed "his step was so light he could wear the same shoes for years, and they always looked new." He was sometimes pedantic, and maybe a little obsessive as he would work out the most efficient method for such repetitive acts as striking a match and would only ever do it that way.

When Bus boarded the train for Paris at the Wilson station in Prague, and from there to Calais and on to London, he had feared he was seeing his parents for the last time. Until that day, they had been a close-knit threesome; when he wasn't with friends he was happy to spend evenings at home immersed in books or listening to concerts on the radio.

In 1938, when Jews were desperately looking for ways to flee Nazi-occupied Vienna and most of my closest Flatter family had either left or were about to leave, the Graumanns in Czechoslovakia didn't believe that they were under an equal threat. Expressions of anti-semitism were less savage than in Austria, even if Czech-speaking Jews were no more popular than the Jews who spoke German and were called "German-lovers". Bob remembered Bus saying "things are going to get hard for us Germans", when in Prague a man he didn't know corrected Bus's Czech.

Klara and Fritz were philosophical about the dangers, and even joked about them. "We thought that Ilka's husband Edgar with his silver pillbox of cyanide pills was ridiculous and melodramatic," said Bus. "But we knew just the same. In the middle of the night we knew we were kidding ourselves." Bus says that as he grew older he understood why his parents had stayed behind. "Young people can look at emigration as a great adventure, but it's not the same for the middle-aged or for old people. To leave behind a lifetime's achievements and to have to learn a new language was too much for them. The young don't know how tired an older person can get."

Wehrmacht troops entered Prague in March 1939, establishing the Protectorates of Bohemia and Moravia. Soon the same Nuremberg laws were being applied as in Germany and Austria. Jews were no longer allowed to work in public employment and the liberal professions, and signs went up in cafés and restaurants banning their custom (*Juden nicht zugänglich*). Jews couldn't go to the woods outside Prague, change address or leave the city limits unless they were emigrating. Public baths and swimming pools were no longer accessible. They couldn't go to Czech schools, ride on trolleys or buses, use the telephone, or own a radio. What those days were like are chillingly told by Czech novelist Jiri Weil in his *Life with a Star*, and in the gut-wrenching short stories of Arnold Lustig.

By October 1941, they would have had to wear the Yellow Star. Emigration was banned and the

Theresienstadt ghetto had been set up as a transit camp. The following year, Prague's Jews were forced to move into tenements in the city's poorest districts. Arthur's sister Ilka and her husband Edgar joined Fritz and Klara and shared a couple of rooms. John wrote, "Klara remained a tower of strength. She sent postcards to my parents in Zurich and signed them *Prochazka*, Still Walking, after the aged Emperor Franz Joseph."

Ilka, Edgar and their youngest son were to be murdered at Sobibor. Their eldest, Fritz, disappeared without trace

At some point, one day, the summons came giving them a few days to put their affairs in order. I suppose they packed their bags with warm clothes and assembled in the old military barracks where they had to fill in forms and hand over any valuables they still had, house keys and identity cards. Then they were put on a train for the three-hour journey to Theresienstadt. Klara sent a last letter from there, and after that nothing more was heard.

In 1994, on one of our visits to Prague, Bob and I visited the Pinkas synagogue that adjoins the ancient Jewish cemetery and is a memorial to the 77,297 Jews from Czechoslovakia who died in concentration camps, out of a population of 92,199 Jews. Two young people were painting the names of these men, women and children in fine gold lettering onto the walls. Bedrich ("Oh yes," said Bob after a moment's hesitation, "of course that was Fritz's name in Czech!") and Klara Graumann (née Flatter) are among the thousands of names, followed by the same date, May 9, 1942.

We went to the Jewish Museum up the street, a down-at-heel office where the shelves were stacked with ledgers and cardboard boxes. One of the ledgers contained the information that Klara and Bedrich Graumann were deported from Theresienstadt in a transport carrying a thousand people to Sobibor in Poland, which had only recently been built. All the transportees died in its gas chambers. Klara and Fritz were both aged 49 when they boarded that train. Four months before, the Germans had launched a massive evacuation of the people in Theresienstadt to other concentration camps.

When we left the museum, Bob recalled that Klara had been so in love with Fritz that Bob, although only a small boy, could feel it. Playing with her one afternoon when Fritz had gone hiking in the Alps, he could sense her grow increasingly tense as darkness fell. Suddenly there was a knock, she leapt up, ran across the room, opened the door and threw herself into her husband's arms. My father felt he was witnessing something rare. The family's nickname for Fritz and Klara was *Turteltauben* (the turtledoves).

Bus had told me he tried not to think about his parents because the grief would annihilate him. He had married, Ilse, the youngest daughter of his parents' good friends in Brno, who had had an embroidery business. After arriving in London two years before Bus, Ilse's father secured the move of his wife and two daughters, and succeeded in getting four heavy sewing machines shipped from his factory in Brno to Britain where he started up his business again. For Bus, these people were his new family.

After Bus and Ilse married in Wales, Bus joined the Czech army-in-exile for the second time to take part in the Normandy landings. He was in a commando unit and was later decorated for bravery, stepping fearlessly through a minefield to save a stranded soldier. "Not being frightened has nothing to do with bravery. If you get shot at every day for months on end, when your friends die or are wounded every day, you just get used to it and stop thinking about it."

The war was over and he was posted to the German-Czech border doing work for British counter-intelligence. He made it clear to me, although he doesn't say so in his memoirs, that he used violence against Nazis, and I'm sure he wasn't the only one to do so. Eventually, each member of his unit was given a week's leave to "go home". When his turn came,

Bus was to be decorated for bravery in the Free Czech Army

he went to Prague with a Czech student partisan who'd said, "You'll need moral support". French soldiers were going in and out of the apartment where he had lived with his parents. The grocers across the street gave him a family photo album and his father's winter coat, which they had kept in safe-keeping. He visited the house where the shoe shop had been. "I made enquiries, but nobody had heard of us. It was a strange feeling."

Later, after he was demobilised, Bus returned to Prague with a view to settling there with Ilse. He didn't hate the Czechs; his enemies were the

Germans and the Austrians. Despite strict food rationing, with fruit and vegetables particularly scarce, it seemed to him that work opportunities were better there than in England.

The first place he went to in Brno was the Graumann shoe shop near the main square. "Our cutter had put his workbench in the main shop on top of the Persian carpet. He had worked for my grandfather, my father and my uncle for many years. 'Graumann'? he said. 'Sorry I don't know the name, you must be mistaken.'"

Bus left disgusted, not wishing to pursue matters further. But it was the Communist Party's growing presence that decided him to return to Britain in the summer of 1946. The West had let the Czechs down, whereas the Russians had come to their rescue and had bravely fought off the Germans. Although the first Russians to arrive in Czechoslovakia after the war were dressed in clean uniforms and were very polite, the next wave came in horse-drawn carts laden with looted goods, and were "rough, nasty and brutish." So Bus made his home in Wales, kept his Czech accent, and never spoke German again.

-27-
1944: Among "the huddled masses"

Taking the train from Miami to New York, Bob was surprised to see no evidence of the war. It seemed remote. "No trains loaded with tanks and guns, no marching soldiers. I didn't realise that despite an intense war effort there were enormous areas of America untouched by soldiery and arms. The country was so vast."

A cousin came to Penn Station to collect Bob and his parents, and took them for lunch at a hotel where couples were dancing to an orchestra playing light music. Emma had been quite taken with the self-assured manner of American women, so unlike the flirtatious Viennese, but this display of light-heartedness seemed inappropriate in the light of Europe's unfolding tragedy. Bob was startled to find that the first sight on driving off Brooklyn Bridge was an ugly warehouse, and not the more fitting public monument one would have expected in Europe.

My grandparents were greatly disappointed by New York. After a short stay in Brooklyn, they moved to an apartment on Central Park West. Having lived comfortably enough in Cuba on Arthur's pension, they found that it didn't stretch far in New York. Emma was hired by a hat maker, while Arthur discovered that Solvay had no real office in New York, and that in any case he couldn't practise law in America. He wrote to his contacts at Solvay asking them to consider him for the company's new set-up in Brazil, but ended up wrapping books in a bookstore until he could stand it no longer. The atmosphere in their cockroach-infested apartment was glum.

Bob visiting his parents in their small flat on the Upper West Side

In her letters to John in London, Emma wrote that New York was a nightmare. The summer heat was worse than in Cuba, the distances enormous, everything was expensive, no one had the time or energy for decent conversation. New Yorkers were the world's poorest people despite all the things they could buy. They were, she said, "proletarians who eat ice cream." My grandparents could not see themselves settling in, and if Arthur had imagined that he might regain some of his former status he soon had to face the fact that this was not to be.

Bob on the other hand, now 17, was enjoying the bustle and energy of New York. "The war viewed from the US seemed far away. There was food rationing but the rations were generous. There was full employment as the young men were in the armed forces and the war industries needed manpower. In America, Japan was viewed more harshly than was Germany." He took a succession of odd jobs while he waited for his call-up papers for the US armed forces. He was a cinema usher at the Roxy Theater, a radio mechanic in a car sales garage and a salesman in a camera store.

With the insensitivity of youth, he told his parents off for being negative and gloomy. "I was upset by their mood. Little did I understand what was going on in their minds - their financial worries, their deep concern for the family that had remained behind, as well as for John in England." Although Arthur admired America, the American way of life was never going to suit him. "He was expected to start at the bottom and work his way up. He couldn't adapt to the back-slapping and the advice to new immigrants. He liked the way I was integrating, but he just couldn't play the game."

When his army papers arrived for transfer to an unknown destination, Bob was quietly relieved to get away from his parents. Arthur accompanied him to Penn station and there he did something he'd never done before: he hugged him. "I was embarrassed," Bob wrote, "although in retrospect the gesture moves me." In later years, Bob - unlike his father - wasn't shy about showing affection. He would hold my hand as we walked together in Vienna, father and adult daughter, which I found slightly embarrassing and yet deeply touching.

Bob was called up in 1944, which guaranteed him American citizenship after a few months' service. He had wanted to be assigned to the army so as to use his languages, but instead was picked by the navy. The recruits were given training in electronics at the Navy Pier in Chicago and then at a naval base in Gulfport, Mississippi, where an officer told them how lucky they were to be learning these skills, as every household would have a TV set after the war. "The soldiers received this information with cold disbelief," Bob notes wryly.

My father's war was uneventful and brief, starting on a refuelling tanker that picked up oil in Texas for ships in the Atlantic; refuelling at sea was dangerous, and required great care. The crew was brutish, except for the man in charge of the mail, who spoke with a British accent and was referred to as "the fucking limey". This man had access to a room at deck level, inside which he played records of Brahms and Beethoven, brewed tea and ate biscuits. Quite often he invited Bob to join him. "Outside, the ruffians banged on the door," Bob wrote. "He identified them by their voices and showed me what he would do with their mail, making the gesture of ripping it to pieces and letting it fly to the four winds."

After a few months, Bob transferred to a destroyer that was to go through the Panama Canal into the Pacific Ocean and then on to China. "I greatly enjoyed the passage through the canal, in

fact my entire time on that ship - the Captain was a civilised individual who had classical music playing on the loudspeakers all day." When the war ended, he disembarked in San Diego, California, to return to the East Coast, thus missing his chance to see China.

Bob as clean-cut US Navy sailor

To put some money aside, Bob extended his stay with the US Navy into the summer, servicing radar equipment at the

Rockefeller Center, as part of a post-war recruitment drive. He was now an American citizen and the GI Bill gave him a year's free dental care, a cheap life insurance policy and three years of free college education. He bought a second-hand Oldsmobile and cruised around New York and New Jersey, and then enrolled at the American University in Washington DC because he fancied a Hungarian girl who was going there. After a bachelor's degree in sociology, he was considering doing his Master's in Paris because of a French sociologist who had impressed him with the finesse of his arguments.

Meanwhile in Europe, John was in love. The object of his passion was a Czech Jewish girl, and they planned to marry and settle in England. Then, out of the blue, came the incredible news that his girlfriend's parents had survived the war hidden by Czech peasants on their farm. In September 1945, John made the short trip across the Channel to Le Havre, which he found in ruins with people living in temporary shelters, and then headed for Munich to work for the American military censorship. His girl was going to Prague, and he planned to join her there as soon as he could.

The train journey from Paris to Munich took a day and two nights because of the damaged rail network, with many stretches that had to be negotiated very slowly. Wherever the train stopped, people gathered outside to catch an apple, a cigarette, something to eat. John wrote to his girlfriend, but mail took three to four weeks, and he couldn't find a quick way of getting to Prague, which was under Soviet occupation.

When he did finally arrive, the girl's father asked John to get him a car, preferably a Mercedes, assuming that he could easily do so as he worked for the Americans. John went back to his job with the American military, aware that he hadn't made a good impression in Prague. The Czech border was mostly closed during 1946, while the Czechs brutally expelled the Sudeten Germans, and a return visit appeared almost impossible. The woman he loved married someone else, but named her baby Jana, after John.

By now it had dawned on John that his father in America was completely lost and had no plans for the future. He had always thought of Arthur as a man who had all the answers. John wrote: "My attitude changed profoundly. Father was a hurt man and needed help. Nobody in New York could understand who and what he had been, or how hurt he was. He needed me." So John applied to emigrate, knowing that he couldn't expect to see his application granted for at least another two years.

In New York, my grandparents had learned about Baron Moritz Von Hirsch, a 19th-century Munich-born Jewish financier and philanthropist who had invested generously in helping Jews from Eastern Europe settle in agricultural colonies in Argentina and elsewhere. Hirsch's fund helped Jewish immigrants long after his death and included a scheme for chicken farms in New Jersey. Poultry farming was considered an easy way to resettle middle-aged Jewish refugees as the down-payments were small, the skills easy to learn and the work not too taxing. In the late 1950s, some 3,000 Jewish farmers produced three quarters of New Jersey's earnings from poultry.

After a year in New York, Emma could imagine herself settling in a quiet backwater to raise chickens and sell eggs. Arthur didn't know what he wanted, but agreed. They bought the farm and five acres of land in Vineland, New Jersey with help from Von Hirsch's Jewish Agricultural Society.

It was while waiting for his immigration papers that John heard about the farm, and he saw this as an ideal solution. "As landless outcasts, herded among the anonymous millions of similarly disowned urbanites, they could never be Americans, and would always pine for what they had lost. They seemed to have realised that the new life meant a change of class and profession." He would join them and become a farmer too. "We will plant cucumbers, potatoes, tomatoes and anything the ground will bear. For the first time since father had left Zurich, I could see a future and a goal."

My grandmother Emma's clapboard chicken farm in Vineland, New Jersey

By the time my grandparents had settled in Vineland, Arthur had had confirmation of the death toll back home: the Nazis had murdered his three siblings as well as cousins, aunts and uncles. He couldn't have found solace in egg farming, as his approach to the world was totally impractical. Unlike Emma, he didn't enjoy getting his hands dirty. Arthur always wore a jacket and tie, even on the farm, while Emma dressed in slacks and men's shirts. For a time, he had a regular slot playing the piano on the local radio station and responding to listeners' requests, which must have been rewarding and was undoubtedly Emma's idea.

Arthur, left, with his brother Ferry who was to jump to his death outside Prague

In London, John had decided to break emotionally from his European past. He would shed his old skin, and he undertook to do so methodically as he waited the 18 months for his immigration papers. His move to the United States meant, he believed, that he had to stop thinking of himself as European. "It implied a drastic self-amputation. Vanishing out of sight of people in Europe who knew what I knew, and entering a land of people who understood none of this, meant that I could never again be what I had been." He said goodbye to his uncles and cousins, not expecting ever to see them again, and boarded the former troop ship USS Marie Tiger.

The ship drew into New York's harbour at night and didn't dock until the next morning, but as soon as it did he spotted Bob waiting for him on the quayside.

"He pointed at me, laughing. Nine years had gone by, each of us had changed a great deal. The world had also changed, and now we touched again." John's recollection gave me another inkling of the physical diffidence that seemed to typify my family. "When I came down the plank we gave each other a vigorous handshake. Then I did something that was not part of our family tradition and it surprised us both. I hugged and kissed him."

To leave post-war Europe was to leave a continent where millions of people were displaced, and families split asunder. John felt the war had destroyed his identity. Once he had had a family, a house, status and citizenship, and these had anchored him in the real world. With all those references gone he concluded that his only salvation would be to find a woman who would understand and reassure him.

He met Hilda Beer in Vineland, where her parents were also chicken farmers. They were Jewish, but eager to shed any links with Judaism, turning to Quakerism instead. She and John married quickly, almost like an arranged marriage. A few days later, the bombshell fell: Arthur and Emma were separating. Hilda felt deeply betrayed, as she had not imagined an unstable backdrop to her husband's already decimated family. Bob was on his way to France, and later told me that his parents' separation had deeply upset him. I imagine that he suddenly felt responsible, now that they no longer had each other to lean on.

When he left for France in 1945 shortly after John's wedding, Bob was 23 and had every intention of returning to the United States. He had given his car to his parents, and with his savings bought an airline ticket. He flew out from a New England air base on a war transport plane filled with other ex-servicemen. Several of the men on board were of Irish descent and were planning to disembark at Dublin when the plane refuelled.

They reached Shannon airport on Ireland's West Coast in the middle of the night. Bob clambered out to stretch his legs and heard a soldier mention visas. He watched the Irish immigration official stamp the American passports. "Do you need a visa to enter Ireland?" he asked. For him, the word visa evoked painful memories.

"Give me your passport," said the man who opened and stamped it. "Now you have a visa."

It was just an entry stamp, but Bob felt that such a hospitable gesture merited acknowledgment and thought he might as well visit Ireland. Then he sailed to Scotland and travelled south through England, visiting his uncles and cousins. He met my Irish mother Aislinn in London at his uncle Otto's house, where she was having her portrait painted, and then went on to Brussels, Paris and Zurich, and finally to Austria. On the train from Zurich to Innsbruck he realised that he might be in for a surprise: the Austrian passengers were greedily eyeing the sandwich he had bought in Switzerland. He was soon to discover how poor Austria had become.

Bob was to stay in Europe, despite the fact that he loved America, while John remained in the United States, although he never felt at home there, working as a United Nations demographer. His deepest conviction, according to his son, my American cousin Frank, was that "purity" was a pretext for wars, and he held the romantic view that in nakedness all humanity was the same. The more mixed blood there was the less the risk of barbarism. John always identified himself as a *mestizo*.

At the end of his memoir, John mentions how much he hated the bullying tone in the song *My Country, 'tis of Thee*, and particularly its patriotic line "Land where my fathers died". Does America, he asks, mean one has to forget one's father? "Mine died in Vienna. His father and his father's father died in Brno." Perhaps John, too, would have preferred to die outside America, but he didn't; he collapsed suddenly at the age of 57 at his home close to New York, even though Europe was in his heart.

-28-

1946: The chicken farm

When still a boy in Vienna, Bob had a dream in which his father had a wooden leg, like so many victims of the First World War. "That dream upset me deeply for many months," he said. Arthur's helplessness in his later years, his self-centred personality, aggravated Bob, and perhaps he also resented him for the intellectual complicity he shared with John, rather than with him.

Vineland, New Jersey, turned out to be unliveable for Arthur, offering no solace to his soul. He suffered deep depressions and health problems. Bob sided with Emma over the breakup. He saw Arthur as selfish and disloyal. It was only much later that he felt he understood his father's frame of mind, and was annoyed with Emma for having hijacked his own feelings.

My grandfather Arthur was to wander but not settle for many years

Now that Bob too is dead, I can't ask him where Arthur went after leaving Emma, but John said he lived like a tramp, by which I suppose he meant that he camped in various people's homes, including those of women with whom he had liaisons.

John's widow, Hilda, didn't have much time for Arthur, considering him a snob and a womaniser. Aislinn, too, found him a trial. He came to Geneva in 1954, the year after I was born, and I have a photograph of me on his lap. He has a fine head of springy white hair, is wearing a dark suit and tie and looking down at me with a smile that brings out his crow's feet. He visited again when I was two years old, staying in a *pension*, my parents' apartment being too small to accommodate him.

He had been offered a job at an international organisation in Geneva, and to my parents' horror planned to settle there permanently. Aislinn's diary for 1956 makes that abundantly clear.

"He is such a demanding person," she wrote. "You can't forget his presence." He would drop by in the morning for his mail, and regularly stay for supper, pontificating darkly about the world. He grumbled a great deal, and was unsympathetic to the problems of anyone other than himself. He complained about loneliness, and about ailments that Aislinn was convinced were psychosomatic.

When Arthur finally left Geneva in March, having resigned from his job, he moved back to Zurich, staying there for a while, and then Vienna where he died in January 1962 with a priest at his side, embittered against life. He had been living with a Jewish-Austrian-Irish woman. I remember that Bob cried when he heard his father had died. I was ten and that was the first time I'd seen my father cry.

Me feeding my grandmother's chickens in New Jersey

Later, much later, Bob felt he understood his father and that he could imagine the conversations they would have had. He wished he hadn't been so prickly and instead had shared more moments of complicity. "I think I knew my father in Vienna as a happy man. His job and his social position gave him a psychological balance that was reflected in his manner. All that was gradually destroyed."

"He was a mediocre father and husband," Bob said. "Someone once suggested that his real nature was that of an artist." Perhaps he could have become a professional musician, although he had enjoyed practising law. His decision in 1942 to resign from his job in Zurich and embark on an uncertain emigration "turned out to be a disaster for him, a mixed blessing for my mother and led to the end of their marriage - the harshness of their fate bringing their fundamental differences to the fore."

Vineland was a bit like a kibbutz without the communal living. The chicken farm's unmaterialistic lifestyle suited Emma, while also offering her educated, German-speaking friends among the other central European refugees. Her days as the wife of a successful Viennese lawyer were over, but she didn't regret them.

I remember the white-painted clapboard bungalow; it had a porch, a yard and a large chicken coop leading into the cellar where the eggs were sorted and stored. The Vineland Egg Auction peaked in 1953, shipping almost a million eggs a day, but the fierce winds of hurricane Hazel the following year destroyed many chicken houses. By the 1960s, most Jewish chicken

Emma looking like a Russian kolkhoz worker

farmers had moved to other parts of the country and into other professions.

I don't know much about Emma's days in Vineland, except that she was shocked and hurt when Arthur left her in 1949, and wrote indignantly to her brothers in England. In a heart-rending letter addressed to Bob several years later, she says she knew that Arthur was deeply unhappy, and was ready to take him back and give him a good home, and could Bob tell him so?

I know of Emma's last years through letters my uncle John wrote to Bob. Chickens, eggs and later piano and singing lessons brought in only a little money, yet somehow Emma managed to save. She never threw anything away, not even pieces of string, rusty nails or food that had gone off. After Arthur died, she received a tiny widow's pension from Solvay.

John visited from New York with his three children - my cousins - but he was always incredibly tense at the thought of seeing his mother, and they all found the drive to Vineland deeply unpleasant. Bob would visit her from Paris every year or so, sometimes accompanied by Lucy and me, or by our two half sisters.

In her mid-seventies, Emma started to lose her memory and would forget the way back from Vineland to her farm. She piled up traffic violations. Her friends grew concerned, and although she was ready to battle on against her growing distractedness they finally convinced her to move to an old people's home. The one selected was in Newark, and its residents were mostly Jewish and German speaking. The neighbourhood was rough and the old people were not encouraged to go out for walks.

John suffered a serious mental collapse in the same year – 1970 – that Emma entered the care home. She had tried to help him - clumsily no doubt, because she hated to see her son in despair. His breakdown was due to many things, and some of it centred on complex feelings about his Jewish roots, which he felt were a form of branding as inescapable as being born into an Indian caste.

The deterioration of Emma's mind may have echoed John's distress, and her memory declined rapidly. Within a month of moving into the home, it seemed unimaginable that she had until then given piano lessons and driven a car. She did remember that she had two sons, and liked to keep their letters near so she could see their handwriting.

John visited her on alternate Saturdays, but he was tackling his own deep sense of alienation. "In the presence of visitors," he wrote, "she is almost invariably cheerful. She does mention, however, that she wakes up every morning at 4am, occupies herself with a few things, and then returns to bed. How she feels, alone and awake in the small hours of the night, she does not specify."

No one told her when her eldest brother Bruno died in England, fearing her reaction. She was losing her English fast. She stopped writing to Bob, although she liked to have signs of life from him. John who felt himself in an equally deep fog visited her in February 1971 and found she had lost touch with reality. "*Sag mir einmal,*" she asked, "*mit wen war ich eigentlich verheiratet?*" Who was I married to? You were married to Arthur Graumann, he replied, and she seemed agreeably surprised.

I gather from John's letters that Bob in Paris was feeling ill at the time, something to do with his gut, and I am sure that eating away inside him was anxiety about his brother and guilt about his mother. He must have felt powerless, as his second marriage was faltering. Emma's own thoughts increasingly took her back to her younger years in Vienna. "She thinks that in the spring she will return to the Wintergasse, and that Klara is alive and waiting for her," John wrote.

Returning to her childhood home in Vienna and seeing her dead sister may also have been Emma's way of facing her own death and perhaps making it bearable. She and Klara would be together again. I hope so. I think her last year or two when her mind had gone were ghastly. She died in November 1972, two years after entering the home, and we don't know where she is buried. A rabbi relative in America tried unsuccessfully to find where her ashes or bones lay. As far as I know, she has left no physical trace.

-29-

2013: Remembering a
mother abandoned

With a Cheshire cat grin spread across his face, my father Bob was one of the hand-painted cardboard children in Otto's puppet theatre. The other, a slim-shouldered boy with downcast eyes and large ears, was his cousin Peter, Otto's son, who lived in Vienna with his mother Eva. Until recently all I knew about Eva was that she was mad and that she had died in a concentration camp. I also knew that Peter had never forgiven his father for not having helped her, his first wife, flee the Nazis.

I first met Peter in Vienna in 2013 when he was a sprightly old gentleman of 88, about the same age Bob would have been. Felix, another elderly cousin of theirs in London, had told me that Peter had written a book about his mother. I found it on Amazon, *My Mother was Viennese*, and reading it was like discovering a secret room in a house-dream. I got in touch with Peter, who suggested I join him in Vienna where he was to do a book presentation. He was staying in the very grand Bristol Hotel next to the opera house, and that's where we met on a spring weekend.

As an adult daughter, I sometimes felt I had to protect Bob, that he had suffered and was highly sensitive; yet I also felt that I didn't always meet with his unconditional approval. I said the wrong things, spoke naively or over-emphatically, and that may have reminded him of what had annoyed him about Aislinn my mother. At least that's what I imagined. Having idealised him for many years, this could be hurtful.

I don't know how Bob would have reacted to Peter's book. I would have liked to discuss it with him, but then again it would have depressed him. I learned from Peter's book that Eva died in February 1944, aged 41, in Auschwitz. She had travelled on the same convoy from Northern Italy as the writer Primo Levy, but unlike him was gassed on arrival.

"To get it out of the way," Peter said walking briskly out of the hotel's lobby into the Kärtner Ring, "I have advanced prostate cancer." In the same abrupt manner, he glanced at me and said that I looked like Bob. He was slim, energetic, dressed in a white summer suit with a striped shirt. I learned that he and his late wife had loved ballroom dancing. It was a sunny weekend, and Vienna's skies were aquamarine. He had bought tickets for the ballet that evening, and before the performance we ate schnitzel and buttered spring potatoes at the Mozart Cafe, accompanied by a pleasantly tart white wine.

Peter was in Vienna to attend a homage to his stepmother Hilde Löwe, who had written music under the name Henry Love, and a presentation of his book, both events being part of a programme about neglected pre-World War Two Jewish creative talent. The renowned tenor Richard Tauber and Marlene Dietrich had sung Hilde's hit *Das Alte Lied*. Hilde's comic operetta *The Window Cleaner of Monte Carlo* was being given a concert performance at the Theater Nestroyhof, once a Jewish theatre and the only Art Nouveau theatre designed by a Jewish architect – Oskar Marmorek. It was in this building that the satirist Karl Kraus had declaimed his texts, and that Zionist leader Theodor Herzl had staged his plays before devoting himself single-mindedly to the quest for a Jewish state.

The night after the ballet, Peter and I went to the concert performance of Hilde's operetta. He laughed a great deal throughout. As I don't speak German, I didn't understand the dialogue or the lyrics in this love story between an actress and a window cleaner, but Peter said they were typical of Otto's sense of humour. "Exactly like the puppet theatre," he said, "the same sense of the absurd." The following afternoon, he talked about his mother to a small, attentive audience of intense older women wearing glasses. He made me feel guilty when he said he had barely slept the night before because of the old memories I had stirred up.

Peter's career as an industrialist producing machine tools in England made him comfortably off, and after retirement he enjoyed sponsoring young musicians and environmental causes. He hadn't had time to have children, he said, but I wondered if the thought of being a parent hadn't been a little scary. Although he was liked and respected in his Sussex village in rural southern England, he felt that being known as Jewish had created an intangible though never rude barrier that marked him out as foreign. As I write, two years have passed since we met and cancer has won the battle.

Thanks to research by an Italian historian, which

Peter relates in his book, I now know what happened to Eva after the Anschluss, where she went and how the Nazis caught up with her. It is through Peter that I also discovered fragments of a far more complex Eva, the mother he barely remembered, no matter how hard he tried, the woman who had been dismissed as crazy.

Eva was the daughter of my great-grandmother Josefine's rich brother Ignatz Haas. As well as chocolate, Ignatz's fortune in the confectionery trade owed much to "silk sweets", a sweet with a soft fruit centre he had discovered in Berlin and copied. He lived with his family in a palatial 35-room residence in Vienna's Mariannengasse, which he had bought from Emperor Franz Joseph's personal physician.

Now the headquarters of Vienna's electricity company, it is in the medical quarter next to the once Jewish Art Nouveau polyclinic, and is so enormous - I counted 91 windows just on one of its two unadorned facades - that it is hard to imagine how one family could have filled all the space. What

Peter and his mother Eva in Italy

was once a beautiful garden at the back has been replaced by a parking lot.

Emma hadn't much liked her two Haas cousins - she found Eva to be impractical and exalted, and Eva's brother a snob who called himself "de Haas" to imply Dutch nobility. Both lived in the vast residence with Peter's grandparents and his great-grandmother, who was an unpretentious soul. In his book, he describes the pungent smell of soap and cheese emanating from the larder to which she had the key. She made the *Harzer* sour milk cheese herself. She also secretly boiled half a pig's head on the gas ring in the bathroom next to her bedroom and ate it all on her own. The result was a turbulent digestion that at times seemed to propel her along the corridors.

The severe building in the Mariannengasse still has an impressive marble staircase (one can glimpse a long marble hall through the wrought-iron entrance gate), and used to boast a scullery, a laundry and a gymnasium, a smoking room with red plush seats, an oak-panelled billiard room, a library and the garden at the back with lilac, acacia and ash trees. By the time Peter was born, a few months before Bob in the summer of 1925, many rooms were no longer in use as the once plentiful staff was reduced to a maid and a cook. The First World War hadn't been kind to the confectionery trade, and Ignatz had had to close many of his shops. Peter remembers roaming the abandoned rooms and corridors, and lifting weights alone in the dusty gym.

Otto was a penniless painter when he married his cousin Eva, and had no choice but to accept the hospitality of his in-laws in the Mariannengasse behemoth. Ignatz gave the young couple a ground-floor duplex bed-sitting room, which had a fountain in one corner; it had been one of the first homes in Vienna to have running water. But Otto soon felt that the world was closing in on him. In the army, he had been an officer in charge of men and now he was being treated like an irresponsible adolescent by a father-in-law who also happened to be his uncle.

Few traces remain of Eva's young life, but Peter recalls that she read a great deal and had a passion for Dostoyevsky, and that her friends were

Viennese blue stockings who didn't work but went to lectures, and espoused causes and exotic cults. After Peter was born by caesarean section, Eva was physically and mentally ill for a long while. By the time Peter was three, Otto no longer lived at home and was asking for a divorce. His mother Josefine was devastated, as she was deeply attached to her brother Ignatz who had always helped her family in times of need. Ignatz must have been very angry with Otto.

Richard, who would often take the moral high ground on family matters, acted as Eva's legal counsel in the divorce proceedings, which concerned Peter's guardianship. Richard in his memoirs mentions how much children suffer when their parents part, and I suppose he was also thinking of Peter. The judge ruled in Eva's favour, allowing Peter to spend every other weekend with his father.

When she recovered, the now single Eva took four-year-old Peter on long journeys through the spas of Austria and Germany, and to Paris and Ostend, Geneva and Merano in Calabria. She spoke fluent Italian, and loved Italian culture and its diet of pasta, vegetables and olive oil. She conveyed this taste for good cuisine to Peter, who was to become an excellent cook. Ostensibly to escape the harsh Viennese winters, these long trips may also

Mother and son on a visit to Paris

have been a way of punishing Otto by keeping Peter out of school and away from him.

Mother and son had a close relationship. The year Otto made the puppet theatre, in 1932, a photograph taken in Paris shows Peter aged seven on his mother's lap, the same age as his puppet figurine, the same pouting lips. Eva's arms are wound around his waist and she looks down, her cheek gently resting on his temple. Peter gazes into the camera lens, one arm tight around his mother's neck, the other slung negligently across her lap. It's a Madonna and child, except the child wants to run off to play.

Peter discovered much later that Eva had kept a diary about him between the ages of three and 12. By this time he was in the south of Wales running a small leather button factory, and his mother had been dead for six years. As he held the slim notebook in his hand, several of his childhood paintings slipped out onto the floor. "The diary told me so much about the mother I had left before I could really get to know her; her humanity, decency, compassion and her remarkable insight into the nature of a child's mind. Above all, the pages of the diary were imbued with a mother's deep love for her son."

The child who Eva evokes must have been a little like herself – anxious, watchful, subject to dark moods. His first word was "angst". But he was also funny, sensuous, turbulent and given to outbursts of affection.

"Sometimes he can be very affectionate and at other times all closeness can be repulsive to him. When he hops into bed with me in the morning and has slept well, he loves to caress me. 'That's my little head, it belongs to me,' and he embraces my neck and sings the words."

"Peter likes smelling – his favourite smell is the billiard room's stale, unlived-in aroma, which he finds delicious. He closes the door behind him and says he must penetrate deeply into the room where he savours the scent alone. Warm May sunshine is streaming into our room today, and Peter says, "it smells hot, it smells of sun."

When Ignatz developed liver cancer in 1934, Eva sent nine-year-old Peter to a boarding school in the village of Grinzing, just outside Vienna. The house did not offer a suitable environment for an emotional child, as her father was in great pain and needed constant nursing. The progressive Landerziehungsheim Grinzing school is deliciously described by George Clare in his autobiography *Last Waltz in Vienna*, where he was a day boy. Because he was too young, Peter was just a boarder and went to the Grinzing elementary school, but the older boarders taught him about sex and drugs. "In particular, I remember the son of a wealthy Bulgarian who seemed to have an unlimited supply of opium cigarettes which he generously shared with his fellow pupils."

A year later Ignatz was dead, and Peter came home to attend a gymnasium in the Glasergasse. On his walk back from school he went past the vaulted sewers made famous by *The Third Man*, quite easily accessible from the embankment and a favourite destination for schoolboys. By now the Mariannengasse mansion needed the sort of upkeep the household couldn't afford; Eva had a small allowance from her mother, which she supplemented by pawning furs and jewellery at the Dorotheum auction house. On Sundays, she and Peter would picnic in the Vienna woods on cheap but delicious goose chitterlings, sausage meat and pickled cucumbers.

Their quiet complicity was to end forever on March 12, 1938, when Nazi troops marched into

Vienna and Eva secured her son's safe journey to London. Shortly after he arrived aged 13 on English shores, Peter was sent to a boarding school in Bromley, Kent, which had special rates for refugees. His mother was seldom in his thoughts while he was busy learning English and making friends.

Eva left Vienna for Italy in April 1939, invited by a Jewish school friend, Käthe Calio, who was married to an Italian musician. She had a three-month visa, and hoped to travel on to London via France. When the visa expired, she stayed on illegally. Her hopes of joining Peter diminished when the Allies declared war on Germany on September 3, and were dashed completely when the Italians declared war on the Allies in June 1940.

Peter was in London when Otto gave him a letter from Eva. "This was the first from outside Austria. She was destitute. She implored me to ask my father for help. I picked up my courage and pleaded with him. He flew into an uncontrollable rage and told me never to broach the subject again. I did not. Perhaps it was cowardly of me, but what could I do and what would have changed his mind? I was thirteen and thoroughly intimidated, knowing no one in what was still a strange country."

He was also certain that they would eventually be reunited. Otto could have signed the documents taking responsibility for Eva, and these would maybe have allowed her to leave Vienna and join their son. Once she had reached Italy, Otto may have assumed that she was out of danger. Perhaps he was lulled into a state of hostile passivity, unsure how he would manage if Eva came to London, where she would have been completely dependent on him.

"How can people come to hate someone they once loved?" Peter asked me in Vienna more than seven decades later, as we sat side by side in the Art Nouveau theatre. I imagine that Eva's fate weighed heavily on Otto's conscience, and that hating her was easier than envisaging a future in the same city. Peter wrote to his mother asking her not to contact Otto directly because she might add to the tension between them. He wrote again twice, but didn't hear from her.

Peter was at St Marylebone Grammar School, following its evacuation from London to the Cornish seaside, when he received the message from the Red Cross reporting his mother missing. "It did not tell me anything new, but it came as a profound shock – the realisation that I had almost lost sight of her in pursuit of my new life. For the first time there was a feeling of guilt because I was safe and my mother was not. At one point I was quite sure she too would be safe with her friend in Italy."

When he left school aged 17 the following year, in 1942, Austrian Peter was an "enemy alien" and as such had four options: the Pioneer Corps – the only army unit open to foreigners – the mines, farming or engineering. After an unpleasant attempt at farming, he opted for engineering and a job with a tool-making company in Surrey where he met his future wife at a dance school.

In early 1946, he received a letter from his mother's friend in Italy, telling him that the Germans had arrested Eva in Arco at the end of 1943, just after Italy had surrendered to the Allies and the Germans had taken control of north and central Italy. She was imprisoned for two months at Trento close to the Dolomites, was taken to Fossoli di Carpi transit camp on February 15, 1944, and on the 22nd was put on the first transport to Auschwitz.

Peter learned about his mother's last months in a book published in 1995 by an Italian historian who was to help set up a memorial in Arco dedicated to Eva and to two other Jews arrested there in December 1943. Their names are inscribed in Hebrew on a plaque affixed to a large Dolomite rock in a park.

Peter with his
stepmother Hilde

"A strong feeling of guilt has remained with me all my life, a guilt that became almost unbearable on reading the detailed account of how she had managed to survive until February 1944 and her terrifying final days at the hands of the Germans." Eva had spent more than four years sharing tight lodgings with Käthe's family in Turin, then at Rizzolaga in Trentino Province. At one point she decided that she could no longer put her friends at risk and moved to the town of Trento, trying to make some money through private tuition. The Italian police kept tabs on foreign Jews and she was first registered in Riva del Garda, then in Arco, a mountain village at one end of Lake Garda.

In her letters to Peter, Käthe expressed how guilty she felt that she had allowed Eva to fend for herself. "If I had conquered a kind of lethargy, a lack of imagination within me, I am sure a secure hiding place would have been my reward." She wrote Peter that Eva had been "one of the wisest and unhappiest beings of all time."

She had spent her last days in a house outside Arco with several families. Aware of her straitened circumstances, an Italian woman had asked her to teach her boys German. On the evening of December 21, the lesson had just begun in the dining room when there was a knock on the door and two SS officers entered. They asked for the *signora*.

"So my mother went down the stairs, across the corridor with arches adorned with green arabesques and, passing through the big gate and along the path of the garden crowded with palm trees, she disappeared into the darkness of the winter night." Eva didn't know that her mother and grandmother had already been killed in Belsen.

Peter visited the house surrounded by a lovely landscape when he went to Arco for the placement of the memorial stone. He was now a successful businessman, a connoisseur of fine wines and good food, a music lover and a charitable benefactor, but had not forgiven his father or himself for having abandoned Eva. "Did I do enough to persuade my unbending father to get his former wife to safety? Was I cowardly, selfish, unfeeling? Why was I spared, and what entitles me to lead this charmed life of mine?"

Otto's drawing of the merciless Nazi maw

In wartime London, Otto had taken up anti-Nazi political cartooning based on his readings of *Mein*

Kampf and Peter says he knew more than most about Hitler's plan to exterminate the Jews. One of his drawings from 1938 showed a long line of men and women entering the open jaw of a huge skull behind a barbed wire fence. "He knew," Peter says.

When Hilde died of cancer in 1976, aged 81, Peter was relieved that Otto opted to soldier on alone in his Elm Tree Road cottage. He would not have been welcome in Peter's home. Peter was planning to express his anger and resentment in 1988 when he visited his dying father in hospital, but his resolve evaporated seeing the old man lying in bed. "It won't be long now," Otto whispered as if to say don't worry, I shan't linger. He died two weeks later. Peter had always admired his father's artistic skills, but he now felt a grudging respect for his toughness and self-sufficiency.

The hospital had asked Otto if he would like to talk to a priest or a rabbi, but he had furiously refused. He wasn't at this stage in his life going to change his mind about the existence of God. "He was a convinced atheist and a fierce anti-Nazi," says Peter, "and had once been a totally integrated Austrian-German who strongly believed that Jews should assimilate."

Peter found Eva's letters in a safe in Otto's cottage, tied up in a neat bundle. He hadn't remembered giving them to his father. In the bundle were two letters he'd never seen, written in Turin in 1939. Eva was ill, destitute and appealing for help. Peter and she had been apart for a year and Italy had declared war on the Allies. Feeling wretched, he read, "That you would leave me in distress, perhaps soon in dire need, in order to avoid difficulties with Papa, hurts me deeply. But I will not write to him since you believe it will make things hard for you."

"Rereading her pleas written in pencil on scraps of paper was painful," said Peter. "It is clear from the very first letter that she had no conception of my father's latent hatred towards her, nor could she have had any idea of the explosion of rage that greeted me each time I asked him to help her. A strong feeling of guilt for not doing more filled my mind."

Peter's book made me realise two things: how easy it is to disappear from memory without a trace, summed up for close posterity in three words like "Eva was mad", but also that I no longer had to filter my family through Bob's sensitivity. I had plunged into his memories and identified closely with him, but this had not given me much space for myself. Bob's dying had freed me to reconstruct my family in my own words, through my own personality, without feeling that I had to seek Bob's blessing or spare his feelings.

-30-
1963: A year in Tel Aviv

As a child, you have to accept change and adapt to it because you have no voice in the decisions adults make. In 1963, my mother Aislinn left my father Bob because she had fallen in love. To complicate things, the man she had fallen in love with lived in Israel. At the time we were settled in a village in the French Jura, a short drive from Geneva where Bob worked for an international organisation. I went to the village school with the local farmers' kids. Grilly is unrecognisable today and is virtually a suburb for Geneva's international set.

I was ten and Lucy five during the year we spent in Tel Aviv. Bob was devastated by the breakup, and moved to Paris to work for Unesco, another international organisation, because he couldn't bear to stay in Geneva. While Aislinn experienced the torments of a doomed love affair, Bob met and married a French woman. I missed Bob so much that tears still come to my eyes when I think of it. When in Tel Aviv I claimed to long for the rhythm of the seasons, and complained about the unchangingly clear Israeli skies, I was really saying that I wanted my father back and my parents together.

Our furnished apartment in Tel Aviv was in a side street on the second floor of a small concrete block with a front balcony, and two bedrooms. Early every morning, wearing shorts, sandals and a canvas hat, I'd walk to school a few streets away, two L-shaped buildings in a sandy courtyard where the children sometimes danced to Israeli songs during the break.

My mother and Lucy in our Tel Aviv apartment

Classes were over by lunchtime, and afternoons were for homework and Hebrew lessons with a round-faced woman by the sea. I'd walk on the shady side of the street to her apartment, and we'd work at a table in her dimly-lit living room, plastic blinds pulled down. When the lesson was over, I'd go in the opposite direction from home, past buildings pock-marked with bullet holes from the guerrilla war of independence against the British, and look down over the wall at the sandy-grey beach.

Born in Palestine to Russian parents, Eviathar was a typical sabra; he had founded a kibbutz in the hills near Jerusalem. To be with Aislinn, he had left his wife and two daughters in Jerusalem, and planned to start a new legal practice in Tel Aviv. He had no idea that his friends would ostracise him, and that the new little girls would remind him painfully of his own daughters.

And there was the added fact that Aislinn was not Jewish. She was blonde and grey-eyed, Nordic-looking if anything. Eviathar warned me that if anyone at school asked if I was Jewish, which no one ever did, I should say that I was. Of course I didn't feel Jewish because we hadn't been raised as Jews; our parents were atheists, and we hadn't been exposed to any form of religion.

Aislinn was the daughter of Ireland's first ambassador, then known as the High Commissioner, who died when I was a baby. She had always been rebellious, angry at injustice, and on the side of the underdog. When she met Bob, she was having her portrait painted by my great-uncle Otto. The Irish ambassadorial residence was just up the road. The Viennese couple charmed her with their stories about Vienna, and their experiences so different from her own. One day, Otto announced that his nephew Bob would be visiting from the United States, and that he hadn't seen him since he was a boy of 12 in Vienna.

Bob was something completely new to Aislinn, with his Viennese accent and his past bathed in an aura of rootlessness and persecution. Later, that accent disappeared but he retained a German rhythm so slight as to be barely identifiable. To Aislinn he seemed tragic and grave, and very different from the Irish civil servant her father would have liked her to marry. They fell in love. Instead of Paris where he had originally intended to study, Bob opted to stay put and do a two-year post-graduate degree at the London School of Economics with a thesis on the cultural assimilation of migrants.

When my parents announced that they intended

to wed, my grandfather may have been disappointed that Bob wasn't Irish, but he didn't mind that he was a Jew; my grandparents were no more anti-semitic than most people and less than some. "Still at least he had been brought up a Catholic," Aislinn wrote. "Poor Bob, he'll starve to death," her mother said, in reference to Aislinn's lack of household skills.

After some hesitation, they chose not to have a Catholic wedding and had a civil ceremony instead in the town hall of the commune of Eaux-Vives in Geneva, where Bob had been hired by the UN's International Labour Office, the ILO. Bob may have tried to convince Aislinn to move back with him to America, but her first reaction was that she didn't want to be so far away from her ageing parents and had no desire anyway to live in "that land of savages". She was 20 years old and Bob 25. They visited Emma on her chicken farm in New Jersey. Richard was living there at the time, but my grandfather Arthur had left.

"I loved the farm," Aislinn wrote, "my mother-in-law's resolute character, the heat, the rye bread with thin honey, Uncle Richard quoting Shakespeare as he graded eggs in the cellar, the supermarkets, the guests who came over to play music in the evenings, Uncle Richard crying as he played the violin, Emma going out into the kitchen to laugh into the roller towel over it. Bob and I slept in the dusty attic upstairs and I was happy. My neurotic drunken family in introspective little England was far away and forgotten. Here was music, sensitive Jewish people from Vienna and Budapest transplanted into rural America and I loved them and felt at home."

I arrived a year and a half later, a screaming little monkey with lots of dark hair born to two immature and isolated young people. Lucy was born five years later. As far as I know, our parents were quite happy together. We lived in a village where in the winter the snow often piled up so high that Bob could stand in the trench he had dug to let out the car and the snow reached his knees. We had crackling fires and roasted chestnuts in the embers. In the summer, our parents entertained friends in the large garden, and we would holiday in the south of France. I went to school across the road, and my French was soon better than my English.

When Aislinn met Eviathar in Geneva through a common friend, he awoke something deep inside her that was strong enough to break up her comfortable marriage. With him she probably believed that life would have more urgency and meaning. She felt that Lucy and I lacked roots, and that we would find an anchorage as Jews. She told Bob she had to leave, and Bob was unable to put up a fight. I know he grieved for us, because he told me so, but he didn't protect us. He didn't know how to, and those weren't times when people spoke of fathers' rights or single-parent fathers.

Aboard the ship to Haifa I read Erich Kärstner's children's book *Lottie and Lisa*, the story of nine-year-old twins who meet after being separated at birth by their divorced parents, and read it again and again.

Aislinn kept diaries, particularly when she was unhappy. She died aged 59, leaving many notebooks filled with her small, round handwriting. Even if I have only dipped into them, I cannot part with them as even unopened they are like a living part of her. Throwing them away would be like killing something. But it was only recently, almost 16 years after she died, that I discovered the slim notebook she had written while in Israel.

At a particularly difficult moment in the relationship, she had written, "I love him and love Israel but they aren't for me. Because I am not a Jew. What right have I to say this land is mine? My relations weren't killed, no one persecuted me. I haven't the remotest claim. The claim that even the most unworthy Jew has, the horridest old lady in the supermarket. The grubby little boy in sidelocks, the hard vulgar young woman in Dizengoff Street. 'Go away, we don't want you,' the lovely land says. Take your anglo-saxon bones elsewhere, descendent of the *herrenvolk*."

The plan for us to be brought up as Jewish girls was never going to work. Eviathar was riddled with guilt towards his own daughters, and we missed our father. It was a painful breakup that broke Aislinn's heart. Pressure from Bob, other pressures from Eviathar, made her take the decision to return to Europe. Brussels was an almost arbitrary choice; Aislinn had a friend there and Bob was not too far away in Paris.

Bob on a weekend visit to Brussels after Israel, with Lucy, left, and me

We arrived one wintry, grey and raining day in late January 1964. "It's all worse than my worst imaginings," Aislinn wrote. "Freezing wind, sooty streets, cobblestones. I feel like a refugee. We stand shivering, stomping our feet, waiting for trams." For the first month or so, we stayed in a hotel, and when the money ran out we camped in an empty flat waiting for the furniture to arrive from Israel. It had only just made it to Haifa. Aislinn took us to a Jewish youth centre where they had Israeli dancing, and I won a book for the speed at which I peeled potatoes.

I don't remember the following incident, but Aislinn recorded it. The first Christmas in Brussels, Bob and his new wife Ariane came to visit. Aislinn had written with artificial frost across the living room window: Happy Christmas and in Hebrew, *Chanukah Tova*. Lucy said, 'Daddy, we're having a Chanukah tree.' Bob was furious. Did he think it was an affectation, and that Aislinn had done this to provoke him? Did he feel she was adding to our confusion? Did he hate this Jewish obsession of Aislinn's, as though she expected him to be more Jewish than he had ever felt or wanted to feel?

Among Aislinn's papers I found a couple of paragraphs written after attending the Passover Seder feast at Brussels' liberal synagogue. It says something about her sense of alienation. She looks out the window and sees a man on the rooftop.

"She did nothing," she wrote. "This was a scene she had gone over mentally again and again. She would be held by terrorists and would have a chance to escape by saying she was not a Jew. And she would not say it. So they would kill her. At least there will have been some point to my life, she thought.'"

Why was Aislinn so attached to Judaism? Why should her identity have to depend upon a lie? And what did being a Jew mean to her anyway?

Somewhere she explained that she had transferred her father's stories of romantic Irish nationalism to Israel because Ireland had disappointed her, and then Israel rejected her. We had a mother who wanted us to be Jews, and a father who didn't see any reason for us to feel Jewish.

Because I didn't know him as well, not having lived long enough in the same home, not having been given the time to grow away from him, Bob was much more of a closed book to me than Aislinn. I created an imaginary, idealised Bob, but did I really know him? Why hadn't he fought for us? Why did he never buy a house, even though he could have afforded one? Why did he leave so few things behind when he died? Couldn't he have had something of the wandering Jew inside him?

Sometimes the death of someone you love can be liberating, and this turned out to be the case for me. As I dug into my family's stories with my bare hands, squelching their lives through my fingers, making them adhere into something that made sense to me, I no longer felt Bob's quiet disapproval of my tone, my intrusiveness, my debatable right to adopt these people as my own.

When he used to tell me about his childhood, I had a palpable feeling of the little boy he had once been. In many ways, I felt closer to that little boy than to the grown man. I also felt very close to him physically, almost as though he had given birth to me more than Aislinn had. Throughout his life, Bob had played an unintentional game of hide-and-seek, talking about the war, avoiding it, talking about Jews, not mentioning them. He hated being labelled, and this adaptable aspect of his personality made him the man he was. And I suppose the way he was has shaped the woman I am.

There are many grey areas in my family's lives, many questions to which I will never know the answers, and the ultimate question is where do I fit in and does it matter? Bob didn't always know where he himself fitted in, but there was one thing in his complicated past he recognised as a gift of fate. "I was a witness to the end of a uniquely fertile period in European history. Of course I was young and stood on the sidelines, but there was something in the air, something that made me feel I had witnessed a peak of civilisation that lasted until the Anschluss. And being a Jew was part of that."

-31-

1974: Safe in England,
but never English

Photographs of the young Flatters before the First World War show them posing in the back garden of Vienna's Wintergasse in front of a trellised shed. Otto is the embodiment of the artist as tortured soul, sulky of mien, curly-haired, wearing a painter's smock. When that photo was taken, Siegmund was alive and Otto's life lay ahead of him. By the time he wrote his memoirs, he was an old man in London. I wonder what he thought about the path his destiny had taken.

Otto was a gifted if traditional artist. My cousin Frank in Philadelphia, uncle John's eldest son, has many of his drawings and paintings. Others have been lost, thrown away, or destroyed in the turmoil of war. Once in a while they appear in a sale. Peter sold several at auction when he emptied his father's studio, including a wonderful full-length portrait of a blonde dancer in a black leotard, and a mellow portrait in browns and greys of my great-grandmother Josefine.

Many of the works depict family members, but not all of them. I have a painting of the Moravian village of Lomnice with its distinctive castle, baroque church and luxuriant hills and trees, an English seascape and an English forest, a charming pencil sketch of an immediately recognisable baby Bob in rompers and a watercolour of a girl on a hill in a high wind. I bought three in England from the executor handling Peter's estate. They were cheap, as Otto is not well known.

In London, Otto and Hilde had soon created a small coterie of actors, painters and musician friends. The Aeolian Quartet liked to use their studio for rehearsals, and Otto painted the Welsh stage actor and director Emlyn Williams as Richard III, the orientalist Sir Denison Ross who was the first director of London University's School of Oriental and African Studies, tenor Rudolf Schock, and the Austrian diplomat and anti-Nazi Sir George Frankenstein.

But over the years Otto painted less and less, concentrating instead on restoring old paintings he picked up in antique shops. He struck it lucky on one occasion when he chanced upon a portrait of Mary Stuart from the studio of Jean Clouet that had once belonged to the Prado in Madrid. He was a proud man, and disliked needing help, as he had in Vienna when his most faithful customers were his older brother Bruno, my grandfather Arthur and a handful of better-off friends.

Bruno used to find jobs for him. Otto tells a story about one of his sitters that reveals his gift for self-deprecating irony. This man - "a small-town tycoon, a reputed miser" – refused to pay for his portrait because he said it was not a fair representation. In court, he told the judge it made him look "like an onion with a beard attached." "An observation not entirely unjustified," Otto commented. In the small town that was obviously Brno, the judge got up from his seat and looked at the frameless portrait on the table.

"It looked awful," Otto wrote, "and I was very much ashamed of it." The judge then observed: "I know the gentleman portrayed here. I see him when passing Liberty Square nearly every afternoon playing cards behind the window of the coffee house." The defendant admitted that he did indeed frequent that coffee house, so the judge said: "The likeness has thus been established beyond a doubt." Turning to the man, he handed down his verdict: "Having chosen this artist from the many in the trade, you have now to accept his opinion of you." Otto received his payment.

Otto believed that an artist should apply his own particular "rhythm" to the world as he perceives it, and technique was about acquiring that rhythm. Think how differently Rembrandt or Rubens would have portrayed the same man, he says, yet both portraits might have appeared true to their models. This personal rhythm, Otto believed, is shaped in the mother's womb by her heartbeat and by the genetic memory made up of the experiences of previous generations. How else, he asks, would Mozart and Shakespeare have been geniuses so early on in their short lives? This view reflects, I feel, a harmonious view of his antecedents, and a belief in generational transmission that I believe I share.

Hilde composed light music in Vienna under the name Henry Love

For a while after the First World War, Otto felt that his beloved Old Masters didn't make sense anymore, and that a more urgent and aggressive artistic expression was needed, but he soon rediscovered their inner wisdom. When he visited England in 1934 ostensibly to prepare for classes he was to give in Brno on English painting, but really to feel out the place, he was particularly impressed by the works of Gainsborough and Constable. When the couple prepared for the move, Otto packed the cardboard puppet theatre among momentos from his past. He could so easily have thrown it away, but instead he chose to bring it along. Did he keep it in a drawer? In a folder in the studio? Did he ever think back to those earlier carefree days?

Weekend parties in those pre-war British years took place at the stately home of Hilde's singer patron, Molly Miller-Mundy. It was an 18th-century Hampshire landmark known as Aspley Hall where Otto "listened to tales about racing, riding, shooting, joined the ritual of the dinner table, remained with the gentlemen to drink port and smoke cigars when the ladies retired. With my hosts I inspected gardens, conservatories, stables and fields, and visited the owners of neighbouring estates." He adds: "No wonder that I, who had made no contribution whatsoever to deserve such generous hospitality, felt an intruder." Among his recurrent dreams was one of being a hotel guest in a foreign land who couldn't pay his bill and had to sneak into his room every night under cover of darkness.

Hilde was the main breadwinner, although she didn't have a work permit, and until the war she toured Europe with singers and instrumentalists, and worked as a music coach. Her career as a composer had been cut short by the Nazis, and the dissolution of many music publishing firms in Germany and Austria meant that she had no control over her songs' copyright. She fought a long battle to be acknowledged as the composer of some of the music to *The Third Man*, including a tune she had written in the 1920s that was used as the *Zither Song* and for which Anton Caras got the credit. She won and was paid yearly royalties.

Otto launched into political cartooning in 1938 after reading *Mein Kampf*, in which the future Fuhrer expressed his hatred of Jews, even if he didn't spell out genocide. He produced 600 pen-and-ink drawings in the hope of awakening the British public to the crimes the Nazis were already committing, knowing that few in England had actually read *Mein Kampf*. He wanted to show them the ignorance, cynicism and brutality contained within its pages. The proceeds from his touring exhibition series *Mein Kampf Illustrated or the Life of Hitler* went to war charities.

The meaning of painting had eluded Otto for a while but now his hand knew where it was going and it was driven by loathing. "It took concrete shape before my eyes," he explained. "I crept into my adversaries' skin, I drew, hanged and quartered them." A man at the Ministry of Information told Otto "that the English didn't hate the Germans as much as I did".

That changed, he said, when bombs started to fall on London and his cartoons were soon in demand from newspapers. Winston Churchill had one of them framed and put up on a wall in his war room; it showed John Bull, the symbol of England, knee-deep in the English channel pulling behind him a flotilla of small boats away from the beaches of Dunkirk.

For a year and a half after his detention in 1940 as an enemy alien, and for the next year and a half, Otto did five drawings a week for the War Ministry to illustrate propaganda leaflets dropped on German soldiers. The war propaganda efforts involved, among other things, dropping millions of leaflets from hydrogen balloons and airplanes over German lines in the hope that these would shake enemy morale.

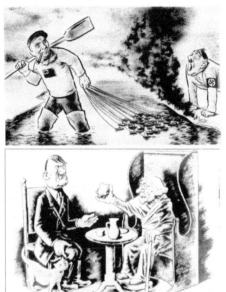

Otto's John Bull cartoon, above, and another anti-Hitlerian drawing

I wonder how many soldiers actually studied these drawings cast from the skies. The operations were a serious investment of time and energy requiring tight planning with rules about sizes, quantities, time of day and influence of the weather. Maybe a few soldiers looked at them and wondered who would win the war.

In 1946, Otto asked the Ministry of Information if he could attend the Nuremberg Trials. Wearing a captain's uniform, he spent three weeks sketching the Nazi leaders in the dock. "I wanted to see these men in the flesh. I had neither hatred nor pity for them. They looked like marionettes forsaken by their master." He was seated far back in the press gallery and needed binoculars to draw the features of Hermann Göring, Rudolf Hess, Hans Frank, Joachim von Ribbentrop and the others.

"I had expected to see unrepentant Nazi fanatics ready to die heroically for their creed, their deeds, their Führer," he wrote in the mass circulation Sunday paper the *News of the World*. "I had prepared myself to draw the faces of tyrants, bullies and sadists; my pencil was to be the sword to slay them. What I saw was a band of timid, dejected men, the plea for mercy inscribed on their faces. I had to remember how these men had once claimed to be supermen entitled to exterminate like vermin people they claimed to regard as inferior." He could hear what they were saying to each other during the break, which was mostly about blaming the Bolsheviks for everything that had happened.

Otto was at Nuremberg where he sketched the Nazis on trial, here Hermann Göring and Rudolf Hess

In the evening, back at his hotel, Otto used the sketches as the basis for large watercolours of the men who had contributed to the murder of his sister Klara and countless family members and friends.

I believe Otto was haunted by a permanent feeling of failure, of having made the grade neither as an artist nor as a man. In his memoir in a chapter about the elderly, he offers a glimpse into his mind. No, he wrote, old people don't lose their mental acuity. "If old people prove to be less materially productive, the reason is a psychological one. Who has not had to learn that his work did not find the response he expected, who has not accumulated contempt for the way he has faced the problems of life?"

The Nazis had killed many of the friends he had loved, and his grief was deep and constant. "Horror gnaws at my heart and though I work and live out my lease of nature, I cannot forget." No matter how light and joyous the superficial melody in his life could sometimes be, Otto wrote, underscoring it all there was always the terrible grinding sound of pain and destruction.

-32-

Forgiveness

Throughout the war Bob had thought obsessively about his schoolmaster in Klosterneuburg. This man, whose name was Richard Zinnecker, had taught him for three grades, from the ages of seven to ten, and in Bob's mind he was the embodiment of Nazism. He didn't beat the school's handful of middle-class boys, like Bob, but thrashed and humiliated the poor. Bob said this behaviour would not have been tolerated in socialist, progressive Vienna.

After the war Bob was angry, later becoming angry with himself for this anger, for by nature he was more a forgiver than a fighter. He felt ashamed that he had been rude to an anti-Nazi family friend in Vienna who had worked as a railroad engineer during the war. "Why didn't you emigrate?" Bob had asked aggressively. "Every decent person should have left."

Bob put off returning to Vienna. When he finally went in 1949, he found the Viennese grey and hungry. The people he met, friends of the family and strangers, were profoundly demoralised. He looked for surviving relatives and found no one. The worst air raids on Vienna had taken place in

March 1945, destroying a great deal, including the Opera House, and damaging most of the Ring's monumental buildings. The retreating German army had blown up most of the bridges, and later St Stephens Cathedral caught fire and burned down to its shell.

The rubble of war in Vienna

Carol Reed's film *The Third Man* must be the best visual evocation of those bleak post-war years in Vienna when widespread shortages led to black marketeering in which soldiers of the occupying forces played their part. The Viennese so dramatically filmed in black and white with their expressionistic features were all leading members of the Burgtheater, Richard's one-time stage. The Austrian currency was so worthless that people payed with cigarette lighter flints instead.

Bob had planned to seek out Zinnecker to tell him how much he loathed and despised him, and maybe even assault him physically. But the poverty and destruction weakened his resolve. He remembered venturing down the steps of a darkened cellar restaurant because he was hungry. Suddenly the lights went on, he was pulled to a table, a violinist started to play for him, and the owners rushed forward with the menu. It was depressing.

"I knew that I might end up buying him cigarettes or sending food parcels," he wrote and so didn't try to locate him and gradually forgot him.

In the end, it was through his renewed friendship with a classmate from Klosterneuburg, Burkhard Stifter, that he made peace with Austria. Burkhard was the other boy in the classroom whose parents had been comfortably off. He was the great-nephew of the 19th-century Austrian novelist Adalbert who wrote about the reassuring comforts of bourgeois tradition, and is considered to be the quintessential Biedermeier author.

So many Austrians had been enthusiastic Nazis and virulent anti-semites, as were probably many of the boys he had sat next to on his school benches. "You can forgive people by putting yourself in their place," Bob wrote. "How would I have acted in their place at the time? Given their background, circumstances and knowledge, would I have acted differently?"

My father and I used to argue about this. I would say that he would certainly never have hurt other people, but I suppose I didn't understand at the time that he was imagining himself as having been born someone else. And perhaps, no, he did not have it in him to be a heroic person.

Burkhard had been a plump, blond and rather unpleasant boy, totally indifferent to if not amused by the suffering of the poorer boys in their classroom. He was boastful about his father's money. His father was a Galician German who owned a small electrical company that built transformers. During the First World War, he had been made prisoner by the Russians. Burkhard liked to tell stories about how stupid the Russians were, and that they did things like firing rounds of artillery at a single soldier. One day when visiting his sister in Klosterneuburg, Otto asked him irritably, "If they're so stupid, why did we lose the war?"

Burkhard had been a rather brutal boy

After school, Bob and Burkhard played at war between the Austrians and the Russians, and as Burkhard was clumsy he would regularly injure Bob. One day he hit him in the eye, causing it to swell and close by the following morning, another time he pushed him down the stairs; despite this, Bob recognised that he knew a great deal about the sea battles of the First World War and about artillery and tanks.

On that first visit to Vienna after the war, Bob asked after Burkhard and learned that he had been made a prisoner of war in Brittany and that his father, an active Nazi, had been put on trial and sentenced to hard labour cleaning up bomb sites.

Much later, Bob developed a fonder relationship with Vienna and started to visit regularly. One day he picked up the Klosterneuburg phone directory, looked up Stifter, and found that Burkhard still lived at the same address. He wrote from Paris saying that he would like to hear from him. That letter was to turn Burkhard's world upside down and provide Bob with a person to forgive.

Burkhard's widow remembered hearing her husband shout one morning from downstairs, and when she came to the top of the stairs he was livid and holding my father's letter in a trembling hand. "A letter from Bobby!" He wrote a long and affectionate letter back and Bob realised that Burkhard had been deeply attached to him. When he telephoned from Paris, Burkhard was so excited that he bellowed down the line.

Bob and Burkhard, sitting front, the richer boys at Klosterneuburg's elementary school

They met again for the first time in 1989 when they were both in their early sixties. "This is incredible," Burkhard said as he opened the door to his house in Klosterneuburg. They spent the day and the evening together and talked about many things, France and French composers, whom Burkhard loved, and the war. During most of that time, Burkhard had worked in a tank repair shop because he was asthmatic and couldn't fight. Bob always asked the same question to people he met in Vienna of the right age. "Where were you during the attempt on Hitler's life in July 1944?"

"In the tank repair workshop. We had to stand to attention in the barracks. We didn't know what was going on." Bob replied: "You were being mobilised against Hitler, did you know that? The plan was to arrest all SS and Gestapo as soon as Hitler was dead." Burkhard said, "I didn't know. My friends said it was all propaganda and Soviet agents. No one would have dared to say that trying to kill Hitler was a good thing."

Even the unfit were being mobilised by the war's end, and in France Burkhard was ordered to report to a unit in Brittany just before the D-Day landings. He got lost in Brittany and was arrested by Nazi military police, and was lucky the police believed his story because at this stage of the war the German army shot deserters.

There was fighting on all sides, and Burkhard and the soldiers who had arrested him were trapped inside a house, caught between the French and German armies. In a split second, Burkhard made a bolt for the door towards the French troops, waving a handkerchief in surrender. He was sent to work in a coal mine in Lorraine, and became very fond of the French who treated him well. After the war, he took over his father's factory and became treasurer of the local Protestant community.

Bob tried to put himself in Burkhard's shoes. Burkhard's father had been anti-Czech and pro-German and had joined the Nazi Party because it addressed his frustrations as a German-speaker in Czechoslovakia, and Burkhard had been brought up in a military spirit.

After the war, he heard about Nazi crimes and wondered what had happened to Bob. He heard that the family had left for Belgium and he hoped they were alive in some foreign country, although deep down a horrible awareness may have been gnawing away at him: that Bob and his family had been murdered by his Nazi friends.

Until reunited with Bob, Burkhard had entertained a close friendship with a former Wehrmacht officer who told him that the official numbers of people murdered in death camps were wildly exaggerated, and that the Austrians had been unfairly stigmatised after the war. Burkhard asked Bob for news about various Jewish friends and relatives, and Bob told him they were dead. This time Burkhard listened to the story of the concentration camps quite differently. He broke off relations with his Wehrmacht friend, and wrote Bob warm letters. I still have their correspondence.

"He was a real Nazi and he loved me," Bob said. He used Burkhard as a conduit for living a period of history vicariously, in the skin of an ordinary Austrian. "I would have been an officer, and I would have admired the excellent German machinery. When the war broke out, I would have been concerned and might have asked myself questions. But then, who knows?"

Over time their friendship developed far beyond what it had been when they were boys. Bob invited Burkhard to stay with him in Paris, and lent him his seaside apartment in Brittany. "Despite his insensitive nature," Bob wrote, "Burkhard turned out to be highly sensitive in matters of friendship and loyalty." He always visited Burkhard when he went to Vienna and became close to his three sons. They wrote him long letters, and always made themselves available when he visited, as he meant a great deal to them.

Burkhard died suddenly of a heart attack, and Bob went without hesitation to the funeral. It was a Protestant service attended by many people from Klosterneuburg. The pastor had prepared a eulogy about what a kind person Burkhard had been, devoted to the church and with a good sense of humour. And then, he added, there was his incredible joy when he rediscovered a childhood friend he had thought lost forever.

After the ceremony people came up to Bob and shook his hand. Some said they remembered him from school, although Bob didn't believe them. They asked him to come to the Heuringen for wine and sandwiches, but he declined and instead went for *jause* (high tea) with Burkhard's family.

"For me," Bob wrote, "Burkhard became a link with my Austrian childhood and he opened up the possibility of forgiveness. Without him, this would probably have been impossible. He provided the image of the repentant Nazi I needed in order to put myself in his place and to realise how much one depends on one's surroundings, and how easy it is to find oneself on the 'wrong' side."

I think of myself as my father's daughter. I have the same solid build, blue eyes and dark hair. I have the same dry cough. But for me he remains full of mystery and contradictions, and we are probably not as alike as all that. Apart from his looks and Arthur's cough, Bob said he had inherited little from his father. "I am an optimist, I don't worry about the future. I am deeply attached to my wife and children. I am sure that I could wangle my way out of most situations, and that at worst one can always die and what's so dreadful about that?"

There was something solid and gentle about Bob that made people trust him. He would listen attentively to people's stories because he was genuinely interested. He became the confidante of several young men who told him about their complicated love lives, and asked him for advice. I used to tease him about his surrogate sons. He was equally at ease with his earnest intellectual nephews in North America as with his bourgeois French in-laws, although he was less comfortable when these different worlds came together. Perhaps he knew that while he was adaptable he feared others were not.

In his brief and often amusing memoir, he judged himself without indulgence as a damaged man who had long been immature and didn't live up to his professional potential, but with age gained serenity. The landscape he enjoyed in his later years was that of Provence; through the kitchen window he could look out on vineyards and across fields to the blue Mediterranean sea beyond.

I wonder if for a long time my father didn't feel shackled by responsibilities, first to his parents, later to each of his first two wives and to us, his daughters. He recalled a childhood experience on a rented bicycle in the Prater park in Vienna. The feeling, as he pedalled vigorously away from his mother, was of exhilarating freedom.

I recently visited Vienna's enormous Central Cemetery, and it took me a long time to find my great-grandfather Siegmund's tomb in the sprawling Jewish section. Despite having made a note of the row and number where it was meant to be, I wandered back and forth at length through the stone-filled woodland, hares and wild deer darting through the grass.

When at last I found it, I realised that I hadn't been looking for the right kind of memorial. It was much larger than I had expected, and much cleaner because it was in black marble, not pitted and moss-covered stone like the many others half-collapsed into the grass. Almost a century of weather had left no trace on it.

Next to it was the slightly smaller gravestone of his sister Tini, who died hours after him in the next room. And underneath his name were engraved the words *Ein Wahrhaft Guter Mensch* (a truly good man). Aware that no member of my family could have visited this place in decades, I felt a strong connection with Siegmund as in the Jewish tradition I placed a handful of pebbles on the cold dark marble; it was as if a channel had opened up between us. I don't speak his languages – German and Czech – and were I to meet Siegmund today he would undoubtedly feel completely alien to me. But the journey through so many pages written by his children and grandchildren had created a tender feeling of familiarity with this threadbare Moravian orphan who one day brimmed with chutzpah in Vienna with two *groschen* in his pocket.

The author

Brigid Grauman was born in Geneva to an Irish mother and American father. Her childhood was in France, Israel and Belgium, where she became a Brussels-based journalist and for many years was Editor-in-Chief of the English-language weekly news magazine *The Bulletin*. She has interviewed international filmmakers and architects, writers and musicians, and reported on topics as diverse as the Roma, social policy and urban projects for British and American media. An occasional painter, she and her mentor, artist José Roland, have sold a work to Belgium's Ministry of the French Community. This book is inspired by her quarrelsome and very literary Austro-Hungarian family, many of whom were among the Nazis' millions victims.

Me and Bob in Geneva

Cast of characters

Siegmund Flatter: Great-grandfather born to parents in the wool trade in mid 19th-century Moravia, now in the Czech Republic, then the westernmost corner of the Austro-Hungarian Empire. Moved to Vienna as a child apprentice, then served for twelve years in the Austro-Hungarian Army. Opened two brandy bars in a working-class district of Vienna, married and had five children. A keen royalist who was always on the side of the "little man".

Josefine Haas: Great-grandmother, Siegmund's wife. A grocers' daughter from Brno, Moravia, she had thrifty ways and strong principles. She raised their five children, and sometimes helped Siegmund run the bars. Known by her husband as "the counsel for the world's defence", she was immensely proud of her sons.

Emma Flatter-Graumann: Grandmother, Siegmund's youngest child born in Vienna in 1895. Stopped school against her wishes to learn the milliner's trade. Married Arthur Graumann at the end of World War One, and had two sons, John and Robert (Bob). Later ran a chicken farm in America. Died in Jersey City, 1972.

Arthur Graumann: Grandfather, born the son of a shoemaker in Brno in 1889. Moved to Vienna to study law at Vienna University, and married his cousin Emma Flatter. Worked for Belgian chemicals giant Solvay in Vienna, and after the Anschluss in Brussels and Zurich. Emigrated to the United States, but returned to Vienna where he died in 1962.

Robert (Bob) Grauman: My father, born to Emma and Arthur in 1925 during Vienna's years under a socialist administration. Went to a Catholic school in Vienna until the Anschluss. Emigrated to the United States via Brussels, Zurich and Cuba. Graduated in sociology, and worked for the International Labour Office (ILO) in Geneva and Unesco in Paris. Died in 2009. Married three times, and father of four daughters - Brigid, Lucy, Diane and Tessa.

John Grauman: Uncle, born Johannes Wilhelm in Vienna in 1919. Spent World War Two in London, where he studied economics. Emigrated to the United States, where he worked for the United Nations as a demographer. Married Hilda Beer and had two sons - Frank and Thomas - and a daughter, Lisa. Died in 1976, aged 57.

Bruno Flatter: Great-uncle, Siegmund and Josefine's eldest child, born in Vienna in 1889. Married Frieda in Brno, the daughter of a scrapmetal merchant, and worked as a travelling salesman for a varnish firm. Had two sons - Felix and George. The family later settled in the UK, where he died in 1970.

Richard Flatter: Great-uncle, Siegmund and Josefine's second child, born in 1890. A lawyer and playwright, and the foremost translator of Shakespeare into German. Studied at Max Reinhardt's theatre school, and worked with Reinhardt. Wrote anti-Nazi articles for the *Wiener Zeitung*. After living in London for several years, he returned to Vienna where he died in 1960.

Otto Flatter: Siegmund's youngest son, born in 1894. Studied at the Vienna Art Academy, and became a painter in neo-impressionist style. His first wife was his cousin, Eva Haas, with whom he had a son, Peter. Divorced and married Hilde Loewe, a well-known pianist and writer of light music. They left Vienna for London in 1934. Died in 1988, ten years after Hilde.

Peter Flatter: Otto's son, born in Vienna in 1925. Lived with his mother, Eva, until the Anschluss when he joined his father in London. Became an engineer and went into the machine tool industry. Sponsored musicians and green causes. Married an Englishwoman, but they did not have children.

Eva Haas: Josefine's niece and Otto's first wife, born in Vienna, mother of Peter. Daughter of Josefine's rich brother in the confectionary trade, who lost his fortune during the First World War. Fled Vienna for Italy, but was deported to Auschwitz in 1944. Died in Auschwitz aged 41.

Klara Flatter-Graumann: Great-aunt and Emma's big sister, born in 1892. Married Arthur Graumann's brother Fritz, moving to Brno with their son Bus. Tried to leave Czechoslovakia for Bolivia in 1938, but the plan failed. Died in 1942, Sobibor concentration camp.

Fritz Graumann: Great-uncle born in Brno in 1892. Returned to Brno after a few years in Vienna with his wife Klara. Co-ran the family shoeshop, known as Graumann shoes. Moved to Prague to run a second shoeshop. Died in 1942 at Sobibor concentration camp.

Ernest (Bus) Graumann: Ernest, known as Bus, Klara and Fritz's only son, born in Vienna in 1919. Took up competitive swimming in Prague. Was a member of the all-Jewish team that was to take part in the 1936 Olympics. Left Prague for London in 1938 on a short-term visa. Decorated for bravery in the Second World War. In Wales, married a girl from Brno, Ilse Wlach, and set up an embroidery factory. One daughter, Frankie.

Ilona Graumann: Great-aunt, born in Brno in 1895, known as Ilka, only daughter of shoemaker Hermann and Charlotte. Married insurance salesman Edgar Oser with whom she had two sons, Fritz and Georg. They lived in a modernist style villa, and had a wealthy lifestyle until Edgar's company collapsed. The family died in 1942 in Sobibor.

Ferenc Graumann: Born in Brno in 1898, youngest Graumann boy, known as Ferry. Ran the Graumann shoe shops in Brno and Baden-Baden. Divorced his wife with whom he had two sons, Anton and Thomas. Committed suicide in Prague in 1942. His ex-wife and his youngest son died in concentration camps. His other son Tom was on a kindertransport and became a missionary.

CPSIA information can be obtained
at www.ICGtesting.com
Printed in the USA
BVHW041333200121
598221BV00010B/714

9 781697 102154